Copyright © 2024 Optimum Vizhan

OV-MAX PUBLISHING COPYRIGHT NOTICE

© Copyright 2024 Optimum Vizhan
All rights reserved. No part of this publication may be reproduced, stored in retrieval system, or transmitted, in any form or by any means, electronic, mechanical, photocopying, recording, or otherwise, without the written prior permission of the author.

ISBN: 979-8-9921415-3-5 Kindle
ISNB: 979-8-9921415-4-2 Paper
ISBN: 979-8-9921415-5-9 Audible

Library of Congress Control Number: 1-14415208331

Because of the dynamic nature of the internet, any web addresses or links contained in this book may have changed since the publication and may no longer be valid. The views expressed in this work are solely those of the author and do not necessarily reflect the views of the publisher, and the publisher hereby disclaims any responsibility for them.

OV-MAX PUBLISHING (DATE: 12-11-2024)
Cover Design By: Optimum Vizhan
Main Cover Page Photo from Istock

OV-MAX PUBLISHING www.optimumvizhan.com/ovmaxpublishing
North America & International: support@ov-max.com

CONTENTS

Copyright	
Max's and My Signatures	1
Enternalizing Creation	3
Dedication To:	4
Living Tribute to Max:	5
Reflection Moment:	28
2nd Dedication To:	29
Preface	31
In The Beginning Before Anything	37
Creation Spoken into Physical Existence	67
Creation Learning:	95
Debunking the Top Ten	152
How Golden is the Golden Rule?	154
FINAL PHASE	156
FINAL PHASE: Chapter One	158
FINAL PHASE: Chapter Two	161
FINAL PHASE: Chapter Three	165
FINAL PHASE: Chapter Four	175
FINAL PHASE: Chapter Five	177
FINAL PHASE: Chapter Six	178
FINAL PHASE: Chapter Seven	184

FINAL PHASE: Chapter Eight	186
FINAL PHASE: Chapter Nine	197
FINAL PHASE: Chapter Ten	198
Eternal Unconditional Love Creation	222
Final Phase Manual	230
My Final Phase Fasting Mindset	244
Types of Fasting	245
My Final Phase Breathing Mindset	249
Breathing Exercise:	250
My Final Phase Meditating Mindset	251
My Final Phase Self-Centered Love part of the Spirit Detoxing Routine	253
My Final Phase Implementing I	256
My Final Phase Implementing II	258
Time Line Balanced Key Points	262
HONOR AND PRIVILEGE	274
Rosetta Stone of Unconditional Love:	276
In Closing	282
Front and Back Covers	290

MAX'S AND MY SIGNATURES

OPTIMUM VIZHAN

This is Me and Max's Signed Copy Edition.
Later that Day Max transitioned on;
I put coconut oil on Max's Paw
and took a white paper impression,
of his front paw print.
Cleaned it Up with an Editor
so that the Publisher Could Include it
In this Edition.

ENTERNALIZING CREATION

FINAL PHASE

DEDICATION TO:

All the Creation that was
Curious Enough and Drawn to
Unconditional Love; by the Spirit,
to Pursue Something
More than Themselves,
More than Their Lives,
More than Their Passions…
Endless Unconditional Love;
with All of Creation as
Friends and Family
with Each Other,
Eternally.
From the Garden;
through the Near Extinctions,
through the Presence of the Spirit
Physically in Us,
Through the Fullness of
Self-Centered Love and
Through the Transitioning of
this Final Phase.
Congratulations. We Made It!!!

ov

LIVING TRIBUTE TO MAX:

Cooper, Smudge and Betsy Too!

When I heard Max was going to be given away; my core went out for him, big time. My core being, started to cry out for him. It wasn't planned. It just happened instantly. I begged, please let me have him. I will assume all liability. Max is a *Razor Edge* Pitt. Wide body structure; all muscle, ran fast, super cool dance moves and Tons of Unconditional Love Like no Other... over flowing like no other.

Flash backs while writing Max's Living Tribute...

My dog friend before Max, *was a Little Jack Russell named Cooper.* Cooper was originally going to be a gift to my best friend, in the whole wide Universe and Beyond. But due to their living restrictions, I obliged and adopted him as my own. Looking back, I believe He had transitioned on from heart failure due to being overweight. Despite his long hair shedding all the time; he was spunky and insisted, I was in bed at 9:00pm every night. Mind you, He didn't wear a watch and or watch the wall clock. He instinctively knew it was 9:00pm; every day, week, month and year. *He'd looked me in the eye,* to let me know what time IT was. And if he didn't see me moving towards the bedroom, he would let out a spunky bark. Several times. Until I responded with ok or **Not Now** Cooper! Go lay down! He was slow to do so; and would look at me with those eyes, *you need to get your rest – let's go now.*

A lot of awesome times with Cooper. The *highlight* was when Cooper was helping me, write the book *His Life manuscript.* This book combined all four gospel accounts of christ, into one easy reading account. Not removing and or adding words. So now, those four account viewpoints were together; describing the events in more detail. Plus adding recent old testament; the book of acts and revelations, that were in association to christ's life. **Cooper would patiently lay close to me, no matter how long I was putting this book together.** Then someone would stop by to ask me a question, or want to have a conversation with me. Cooper would jump up and start barking at them. In a nice, mature way of saying nope not now. We need to write and finish this book, don't interfere. *We would all laugh. Priceless.*

This went on from the beginning; to the end of writing the book, for thirty plus days. It was impressive; that Cooper was so Consciously Spiritually aware of the significance, that he self-appointed himself to be the responsible watchmen of the project. *Priceless 2.0.*

In his last days looking back; he was looking to the distance a lot, like Max. Like he was seeing the Spiritual Side of Creation. He would get excited like he wanted to go play with them; then right out of the blue, Cooper transitions on. Tore me up. **BIG TIME**. To the point, I shut down for a few months.

Our friendship in this phase of creation, was too fast and too short. I dug a hole to lay his physical body in. At the location in the yard, he loved to sit and watch the neighborhood. I dug it big enough so that I could lay in it with him; and give him one more hug, before covering him over. I was shocked; tore up and couldn't shake that awesome Spiritual Physical Friendship, for quite a while. *My furry Friend, thank you for assisting me in writing that book*: by waking me up in the morning when my alarm clock wouldn't, waking me up when I fell asleep in the chair writing and taking all those play breaks from writing. *Your timing was impeccable.* You put a smile on my face every time I think about it.

THANK YOU, COOPER! PRICELESS!!

My first physical animal, spiritual connection was with Smudge. This takes us back further to when I was a child; in my seventh year my parents surprised me, on a return trip from Florida. My mom would like to visit her mother in Florida; during the winter months, for a week or two. We got to pick from two race dogs, that were English Springer Spaniels. The kennel people would bring one young dog out at a time. Both about two years old. Both were ***dog racing professionally*** and got awards.

My parents looked at me and asked which one do you like? Looking back; this was my first time making the decision, based on how we were spiritually connecting at a deep level. With that; after a second time, Smudge was freely wanting to connect with me. My core confirmed it was him.

His nick name was Smudge, I forget his racing dog name. It might have been something like, Brandy. *Then the previous owners of Smudge, showed us his awards. He got six awards in a four-month span. Four 1st Place winners, one 2nd Place winner and one for Best of Breed.* He owned 1st place like a pro; then go to 2nd place like he was thinking of others, in letting them experience 1st place for themselves. They offered to race him for us, if we were willing to bring him back for the Racing Events. He loved being on the farm. He never raced another day in his life, professionally.

Smudge would check up on all the animals, to make sure they were ok. On the summer weekends; he was diving into the river lake water at my parent's cabin, head first. Yes. Diving head first; looking for the rocks, I would throw in the beach shore line. And then there were times; he would jump out of the fishing boat, and swim to shore. **Lol.** We had at one time, thirty cats on the farm. Smudge loved them all, to the point **he would let the kittens nurse on him. Lol**. Yup, kittens nursing on a dog. It's real. *I saw them with my very own eyes.* He didn't move while they were all nursing on him. He had like four kittens nursing on him at one time. When he was laying down; he would let them play all over him, like he was a jungle gym and best of friends.

He would play with the horses, chickens, roasters and cats like they were all the same species. Their shapes; sizes and how they communicated didn't stop them, from having a good time with each other. Playing with them all, was surreal and a glimpse into eternity.

Time with all the farm animals and smudge went too fast. *Seriously*. Before I knew it, I graduated and moved out. It was hard to leave all that behind. My mom; was tough on me, even though I helped her tons on the farm. She said; since I'm "18" now, I need to start paying her weekly rent to stay. Back then $25.00 a week was a lot of money. So; I sadly left, with a deep pain in my heart, missing all my farm animal friends and Smudge. It's like we were all crushed, by the news and my decision. I could see it in their faces. I'm *crying* right now, as I write this. I would come back from time to time. They were excited to see me; but you could see on their faces, how much they were being neglected. *It tore me up*. BIG TIME!

Why? All that tons of free labor I gave my parents on the farm, taking care of all the animals EVERY Day. Plowing, discing, dragging, planting and packing the land with dad; when he was at his day job. Gardening for mom, mowing the huge yard by push lawn mower – every week. Snow shoveling the long driveway in the winter months. Selling straw bales, while dad was at work. I have no regrets, helping out all that I did. I would do it ALL over without blinking an eye. *Priceless journey*.

A few months after I had to find a home for Betsy. My mother called me again; Smudge is in pain soo much, we are putting him down. You want to bury his body afterwards? *It TORE me up* REAL *bad*. Another one of my childhood furry friends was going under. I wasn't there for him, going through ALL that pain… when he was there for me all my childhood years. I said yes. *I'll bury him.* What day you putting him down? She said, **she didn't even care** where I buried him. Cold. I thought hard on that one. Being a farm that's getting subdivided, while being farmed. Finding a place for him would be hard. If not careful, his burial site would be destroyed easily. *Hmm.* Ok. He loved running the long distances, on the 80-acre farm. Couldn't bury him in the 20-acre woods. Dad didn't own it anymore. He loved running to the spread apart telephone poles on the farm, to check them out. So, I put his body in a wheel barrow. **TORE me up 2.0.** Grabbed a shovel and went to the farthest telephone pole on my parent's property. *The most sobering walk, I ever had with Smudge.* The cancer was really bad, all over Smudge's body. He had to be in a TON of pain. **And I wasn't there for him.** *I'm crying now again, like it was yesterday.*

I was talking to him; like he was there with me, in spirit. I was rationalizing that this was the best place, with the best odds of not getting your physical body's burial site trashed. I laid his physical body in the ground, covered it with dirt. **Thanked him for all the Super Times; we had together in my childhood**, growing up with him like the best of buds. AND looked forward to seeing him again, in the future. *Crying through that whole process.* Our friendship here, was too fast and too short.

Looking back... with Smudge, Betsy and all the other farm animal pets... none of my family never really took care of them, period. It was 100% me. All the way. Except for my dad, he bought all their food and paid for all their shelter expenses. After I left; my parents were in shutdown the farm animals' mode, sell the place and move to the city mode 2.0. It was hard; but fitting that I would be the one, to find a home for Betsy and buried Smudge.

Looking back 2.0... After I was basically lynched to move out; every time I did stop to check up on them, their faces were getting sadder and sadder every time. They were all checking out too. Missing me and being neglected was too much pain, for them to bear any longer. *I'm breaking down and crying now as I write this...* I AM SOO SORRY for being forced to leave and abandoning you all.

Totally Epic! *My furry Friend, thank you for assisting me while I was growing up as a child: doing chores, swimming, comforting me while my parents were having marital problems and becoming a young man. My childhood would have been completely different without you.* Your timing too, was implacable. You put a smile on my face every time I think about it. **THANK YOU, SMUDGE! PRICELESS!!**

Update. This last weekend, I was moved to go down the family heirloom memory lane and **looked closer at Smudge's awards.** Yup, his racing name was written on his biggest award. His official racing name wasn't Brandy. It **was *Sugarbush Hillcrest Punch.*** Completely forgot. And like, wow what a name. Now that we know Smudge's real name, is Sugarbush Hillcrest Punch. And Max's full name is Maximus Houdini Koan; we need to give Cooper a full name. *hmmm.* We'll use Koan as his last name like Max's. So, all we need to do is come up with a middle name for him...

I'm wondering now; Brandy might have been the other dog, we had to choose from...

Update. I was doing more cleaning and sorting through my transitioned parent's containers, of small assorted trinkets. And I was surprise to find Smudges, old license collar metal id tag. *My mother had saved it for over forty years.* Amazing. Would of never have guessed; that I was going to find it, at the time of writing this book. I ended up putting it with his ribbons, in a glass picture frame.

Save this space *for introducing Cooper's Middle Name.* I'm back. *Hillcrest*? That would physically and spiritually connect him with Smudge and Max. His favorite spot in the front yard; was sitting on a raised landscaped rock garden, tree shrub crest area. There he was able to see who was coming and going, from the subdivision. Plus sitting at his key spot beside me; to let those walking by us, not to have a conversation with me while writing. **Cooper Hillcrest Koan it is!**

Update: While hanging out with Smudge today; I had this premonition that he has been hanging out, and following me all my life. I asked him and he went into further details; that he was the one that brought Cooper to me as a little puppy, as well as Max. I got tingling sensations when he said that, and felt in my core that it was all true. **Plus.** Now how we as a family have been synchronizing; so well these last few weeks in healings, break throughs, etc.

And Now Introducing Betsy. Betsy was my first Morgan Quarter Horse. Yup. Being some-what of a classroom socializer in my day. I meet a fellow student, that lived on a farm and was looking for a home for his horse. I said, **ARE YOU SERIOUS?** Yup. I learned from him all the ways on how to take care of horses; food, water troughs, cleaning their hoofs, land to roam, electrical fences, saddles, pitch forking manure, bedding and barn shelter. *I was getting stoked big time.* Now I have to convince my parents, to take the horse as my new big responsibility pet. With the proof of taking care of all the other animals, it didn't take long and we were picking up Betsy. *So excited.* Me and Betsy bonded, just like I did with Smudge.

Betsy was huge. Intimidating, when it came to the idea of horseback riding with Betsy. But one day, I mustered up the courage to try go for a ride with Betsy. With the help of my father, I mounted the saddle that was attached to Betsy's back. She was gently walking around to build my confidence up, so that I could go solo with Betsy.

I was getting more excited; to go horseback riding with Betsy, on the eighty-acre farm. And off we went heading to the twenty-acre woods, on the backside of the farm. Horseback riding that day made it even more beautifier. It was so surreal riding, with my new friend. It's like I didn't want it to ever end. Then we got to the edge of the woods. We circled a tad. Then decided it was time to ride back to the farm house.

As soon as Betsy realized we were heading back to the farm house, the all-beautiful day disappeared instantly. **YUP.** I learned in seconds. She was instantly all in. She was in full, everything she had mode and was galloping in ALL of her full glory.

I instantly learned; there's a HUGE DIFFENCE in wanting to Ride a Horse, and Knowing How to Ride a Horse. It was awesome and scary at the same time. I lost the reigns that helped steer, Betsy in the desired direction I wanted to go. The horn of the saddle, is now banging my groin painfully. To stop the pain; I had to grab the horn of the saddle and pray, I wasn't going to fall off. It felt like for ever to get to the farm house. I was all in now, and had no choice but to hang on for dear life…

And was I going to make it back to the farm house, without any injuries?

Finally, back to the yard of the farm house. Just as I felt relief that the ride was about over. Betsy stopped on dime, and I flew over her neck and head. *I was now going air borne solo.* And my face was coming in fast, to dirt and grass. **Yup, I get to eat dirt for lunch.** Now; not only is my groin in huemence pain, my face joined the pain party too. Lol. I didn't care. I was alive and just had the most bad@ss horse ride of my life.

Back to Finding a New Home for Betsy… Being an "aspiring" young adult man now, left home – the farm -. I got a call one day from my mom; saying they don't want to take care of Betsy, and I need to find a home for her. That tore me up. My best friend. I couldn't afford to take care of her, myself. Let alone have a place for her. So, I start calling around. *I was crying through the whole* *process.* **Then the day came, when I could hug her one last time. I cried.** I felt helpless, that I couldn't be there for her. When all those days she would look forward, to seeing me and us playing together. Gone. Too Fast. Too Short.

Thank you, Betsy, *for knowing how to live life to the fullest and getting me home safe.*

It's amazing to look back and going through all these memories; that the Unconditional Love part of the Spirit allowed us to choose to be together as family, and I didn't even realize it at the time. **Until Max's transitioning.**

Ok. PLUS; All these Flash Backs in my mind, has made my friendship with Max all the more-deeper…

Max's Vision as a Puppy was distorted to the point; he couldn't walk up stair steps to get to our bedroom, so I carried him. One day, I showed him how to do just one step. It still was awkward for him. He was strong, ran hard and everything else like a normal dog. But his depth perception, on going upstairs was zero. It took a few weeks and he was finally able, to do one step by himself. **We celebrated!** This was a huge accomplishment for Max. I said it's ok, Max. We'll do one step at a time. I picked him up and carried him the rest of the way.

Now looking back; Max you smoothie you, you were teaching me how to slow down and take one step at time. Weren't you?

After a couple of seasons went by; Max was running up the steps, like he was a pro. Then boom, out of nowhere he busted out in dance moves like no other. My whole face was a big smile.

At an Early Age Max, loved chasing the squirrels just for fun. He would use various strategies. Every time the squirrels would out fox him. Ha. **Out squirrel him.** One time when Max forgot he was on a leash, busted out hauling his body as fast as he could. I was about 20 feet away, yelling Max – no NO. **NO MAX!!!** Max didn't care. He was so close to that squirrel, he could smell it. Then boom. His body flipped on his back and his head and rear switched spots. His body was about four to five in the air. Temporarily suspend, then fell to the ground. **I was in shock.** I was running as fast as I could; to see if he didn't break his neck from the velocity, and the collar around his neck. *I was crying and saying no, no, no. no please Unconditional Love.* ***NO!*** He was motionless. I took off his collar and held him, to comfort him. After the shock wore off; he slowly got up and moved around, like everything was working on his body. Other than being a little sore around the neck.

Max Loved Swimming in the lake water. And pulling the rope hooked to the inner tube inner tube; my grandson was laying on, around in the beach water.

Max Getting Mange. There was a two-year window when I was on seven days with my day job, plus doing my own chores and checking up on family. The Me and Max time was very little; other than taking short walks and bed time. Max is an all-in like to be with people dog, and **it was getting to him**. I tried to redial my days to spend more me time with Max, but it still wasn't enough. He ended up losing all the fur on his back, belly and hind legs.

I wasn't the type *of guy who trusts others to take care of me or my animals.* I used a variety of essential oils; vitamin D in his water, pico silver on his skin, a lot of slow gentle hugging, cut back on work hours and helping family. Max snapped right out of it within three months. His fur was growing back. **We celebrated a lot.** It took him overall, little over a six-month period. He had a few scars left over; as a reminder to me, to put our friendship first.

Max and Car Rides. He loved sitting in the passenger seat, like he was a real live human. People would have to take a second look, wait that's not a human. That's a dog, then they would wave and laugh. When I would make a quick "pit" stop at the store; he would be sitting in the driver seat, *like he was going to do all the driving for us.* Priceless. **He was the man.** We looked for squirrels every time, we went driving in neighborhood settings. Max was all in. He saved a few dogs; who were wondering in the road, by getting their attention. While I was driving very very slowly; to warn traffic and for Max to talk to them, to get them to walk off the road. There was a few of them, who wanted to go for a ride with us. LOL.

All I had to say was "Car Ride" and boom, Max would take a quick piss and jumped in the car. I didn't have to ask him twice.

Instead of Barking; he would do a nnnnn nnnn to get people's attention, to want to interact with them. *It actually worked...* where they thought it was cute. Getting success with that; he branched out with, communicating with the squirrels. ***Seriously.*** He was schooling me again; like with taking one step at a time, to enjoy the experience together.

Very Adventurous. Max was always pushing his limits, on where he wanted to go. Sometimes he saw a squirrel and hauled off running so fast, he would end up in someone else's yard. He would be smiling ear to ear. *Like yah.* That felt good. Then I would have to give this look like Max, we need to stay in our yard bro. No matter how hard I trained him to stay in the yard, he was always wanting to GO everywhere.

Max loves people, animals and all of creation. I believe Max loved animals, people and life so much. That if I let Max go; he would of just keep going and going, making sure everyone was ok. I would look at him every day... "**We're One Day Closer**" Max; where we won't have to worry about borders, collars and leashes, ever again. Never Ever Again!

Making Sure Everyone is Ok. Max would go around through out the day and night checking up on everyone, to see if they are ok. Lay close by; lay by a door and lay by the glass sliding door to check up, on the animals that walk by.

His First Pet Stuff Toy, he would treat it as though it was his very own baby. Max would take his new baby outside with him. Lay him down. Do his deeds and go back to pick up his baby, to go inside the house. Sometimes he took his baby with him, where ever went in the yard. Even when he would hop the fence and walk around in the woods. He would make sure his baby, was in bed with him. One time; he forgot his baby and he started to do, his nnnnnn nnnnn nnnn. I would say, "Let's go find your baby!" He would run over to the door to go outside; and sure enough his baby was right there, where he laid him to go do his deed.

Coming Home Seeing Each Other Party Dance. No matter what I had to do; out away from home, I would try to keep it as brief as I could. I knew Max was home waiting patiently for me. Sometimes waiting 9 to 13 hrs a day. Sometimes I could make a quick pitstop home and take him with me, pending how hot it was outside and or if it was raining. No matter how long it was; when he heard me pulling up in the driveway, he would be waiting at the door.

I would put the key in the door knob and open the door slowly. Max is waiting to see my face. When our eyes locked on each other eyes, he would bust out in the hardest butt tail wagging dance ever. With the biggest smile on his face. He was all in, with every wagging butt tail dance move he did. I would start to teary eye up and bust out in a hard dance move too.

BUT Max would always out do me, no matter what I tried. Then I would slow down and cry. **NO ONE IN MY ENTIRE LIFE**…EVER, WAS THAT HAPPY TO SEE ME COME HOME. DAY AFTER DAY, YEAR AFTER YEAR. PRICELESS.

I would slow my dance down, reach under his belly to see if he was holding his pee. Most the time he was; and so we would grab his treats and head outside to pee on anything, that was a plant. Well sometimes a few tires, pending who was parking in the driveway.

Max, knew how to genuinely love me unconditionally **ALL** the time. And his ALL-IN dance moves when I came through that door; was the icing on the cake, in our friendship. Every one of his welcome home dance wagging butt tail moves, his whole body was into them 100%+. *Left me speechless*; in tears, smiling, at awe that he made me feel that special...**every time**. No one has ever done that in my entire life. **Completely** blown away. *I'm crying while writing and thinking about this again.*

Hard to Say Goodbyes. Long. It was tough to leave home every time. I would start early enough to let Max know; I was going to miss him, like no other. Went outside to do his deeds. Extra rubs and hugs. Then I couldn't stay any longer or I would be late. I would look Max in the eyes; with my index finger pointing up and tell him, "We're One More Day Closer Max, to Being Together All the Time!" Then his face would get really sad, and he would lay his head down. Where ever he was laying down. I would act like everything is ok. Then when in my car; I would start to cry, wishing I didn't have to leave.

He Would Grab a Towel, to get me to chase him. That would be the easy part. After the first few times; I realized, he didn't want me to chase him. BUT to play, who can out tug the other one. He was all muscle and I was all… hmm. Max already knows he won. Ok, to make this interesting for the both of us. I will at least try. Lol. I pulled so hard; it still didn't matter. Max was walking away and the towel being ripped to shreds. Yup. There goes one towel.

Max was proud of himself, that he got me up off my butt to play with him. And have a blast at it. Next day. Shredded towel number two. Next day after the next day. Shredded towel number three. Ok we know how this ends. We need to change the dynamics of the game here, to cut down the towel collateral damage. **New strategy.** I got the shredded towel and start spinning it in circles; to make it look like a mini shredded towel tornado, that Max had to try to take from me. *Nice it's working.* Max is feeling a tad challenged on this one. He sits and observes for the key moment, to take the mini spinning shredded towel from me. I'm smiling.

Bam. He lunges into the air to snag it. I lifted it even higher. He looked at me like. Wait? That's not fair. Your taller than me, *look on his face was priceless.* **Next day.** Same results. Next day after the next day. Same results...

Max doesn't jump this time. He just watches me be entertaining myself. **Brilliant tactic Max.** After a few times; I went back to letting Max get the satisfaction, he was the Master at Shredding Towels. His facial expressions were priceless 2.0.

Stopped using towels for obvious reasons. Then one day; Max sees the hand kitchen towel, hanging off the ledge of the counter. I was to busy preparing dinner for us. **BAM.** He lunges and snags it from the counter. *Hmm.* I should of guest. But was somewhat addicted in playing the game with Max, myself. *I Chase Max.* He lets me catch him and we play who can out tug the other.

It went from full body towels; to hand towels, to gloves, to hats. It was cute and we had a blast. The coolest; *I should say* the COLDEST, was went I was trying to shovel the snow out of the driveway. Max would try to take my glove right off my hand – while I was shoveling. **YES.** And he was good at it. *Like he was a Tibetan Monk of Hand Glove Snatching.* He was so good at it; I can see him teaching a class on it.

Rip Open Packages. Max was always trying to help out. Feeding the squirrels his treats; being a body guard for a toddler, making sure the neighbor dogs felt welcomed, driving the car and yup you quest it… opening packages. He didn't waste any time. He'd look at me like is this package ours? He didn't even wait for me to utter one word, let alone one sound. He saw it on my face.

If there was anything like a Rip Open a Package Competition, Max would be the winner every time. I didn't go for and or believe getting his nails cut. I watched them closely and noticed at some point they stop growing. There is no need to trim dog's nails. Think about it. Do you see any of the animals living in the "wild" needing or wanting their nails trim? **Hmm.** Didn't think so. Last time I was walking in the woods, I did not see any nail salons for animals.

Ok. So, Max has all his nails ripping the boxes open within one flat minute. Pulls the items out and goes for the plastic bubble wrap. His all-time favorite toy to play with. This topped shredding towels and sneaking away with my gloves. He would pop the bubble wrap. If that didn't work, his second choice was to try shred it with his claws. I would get "lucky" sometimes and start popping the bubbles myself. **But it wasn't long** Max showed me a new routine, on how he can take them away from me. Ooooo. You are creative Max!

Try to Climb the Trees. Max loved being with the squirrels so much; he was convinced, he could run up the tree trunks and play with them. Running on all the branches; and hopping from branch to branch, just like they do. If they can do it then so can I … was so deeply in his spirit. He would jump as high in the air as he could; at the bottom of the tree, the squirrels just ran up. *He was all in* on his face. The way his body was jumping, he completely believed he could. After a few attempts, he would give up. Next day, he went through the same process. **BUT**, tried a little harder. Tweaked his technique. He was dedicated to believing; he was going to be able to run with the squirrels, from branch to branch. Priceless. After a few weeks of attempts, he accepted it and moved on to the next interesting experience with creation. Once in a while; Max would stand up at the trunk of the tree, with his front paws leaning on the tree. And the look in his eyes; one of these days, I'll be running on those tree branches.

Help me Mow the Yard. Out of the blue, Max would start supervising me while I was mowing. *Oops.* We were mowing the yard together. Max would walk by me at the same pace; on the side he was going to lean on me, to go into a certain direction. Like he would lean on my right side, to get me to go to the left. It was priceless to see how much, he was into mowing the yard with me. When we would get done mowing the yard; we would take a break by sitting down in the front lawn. I would give him a Thank You treat, while watching the traffic and people go by. A Surreal feeling, being connected that deep as friends.

Chase Snowballs and Dig for Them. Even though Max like to lick and bite at the snow piles, *he loved his snow balls even more.* As soon as he saw me reaching down to make a snow ball, he was all in. Like a baseball player; catching a pop fly baseball, falling from the sky. If in his excitement missed the pop fly; then he would go diving head first, into the snow to get the snow ball. Sometimes he couldn't find it. So, he would start nosing around for it under the snow surface. *It didn't matter the size*; it was a snow ball and he wanted to eat it.

Sneak out Pass the Area then Double Back. Max loved connecting with creation big time. To the point; he was always trying to get closer, to whoever he was trying to connect with. Living in a subdivision of homes; on the back side of a wooded lot, gave Max a lot of options any time of the day. Max's stature was big, thick and muscley.

Some people and animals were apprehensive to engage with Max. So; we had to teach him to do soft intros, with people and animals. He learned to wage his tag; stand and or sit still until the people or animals, moved towards him. **BUT**. His excitement to connect would most of the time win out. Max being on a 30-foot leash; I was always ready for the workout, that was about to happen.

When Max decided, he was going to get friendly and connect with them. I had to positioned myself, to hold him back from getting closer. This took all my might and determination. It felt like I was at the gym, getting a good hard workout for free. This was the back ground to how **Max, develop a very clever technique**. Max would walk away, from the people and animals he wanted to connect with. Once he got the rope length he needed, then he would make his way towards them. While watching me with one eye, to see if I was paying attention. He was slow and gentle. And before I knew it, he was connecting with the person and or animal. It took me several times, before it sunk in how clever Max was.

Brillant on his part. Taking all those elements of trying to connect in the past; the length of the rope and the timing to reach his desired goal, in a peaceful fluid way.

Love Little Children. Max would *instantly* be their body guard. He would always start out beside me; and once he felt at peace that I was ok, he would move around to see how everyone is doing. But if a child entered the room and or area. Max would immediately stop hanging out with me and or others in the space, and go straight to the child. His tail would be wagging full on. He would follow that child around, every where the child would go. Max would give the child room to go where they wanted to, but close enough to help if needed. If I let him, he would even go home with child if he could. Thoroughly impressed, how Max automatically was looking out for the child. **Every time,** like clockwork. He knew exactly what to do in every situation, like he instinctively comprehended their need.

Play with Neighbor Dogs. This was one of his favorite things; when we were on our walks in the woods, and if the neighbor dogs came into our yard. Max's tail would be wagging so hard, as he saw anyone of them coming his way. If Max wagged any harder; I wouldn't have been surprised, he would of started flying like a helicopter dog. Yup! *They would* do their smelling each other greets, like it was the first time they met. Take turns peeing on the same plants. Playing with each other like they were best buds. The enthusiasm of seeing each other, each time *was always firing* on all cylinders.

Max let me Know Peeing on Objects was a Communication Network of saying, hi to each other. I was told repeatedly throughout my life; that animals are territorial and they mark their territories, by leaving their urine on objects… And like any pieces of information; if heard enough times without doing actual research on, it becomes automatically believable. *That alone should be a concern right there,* but it's easier just to believe. Besides everyone else is saying it too. They all can't be wrong? This is common throughout the Creation Learning Phase.

But Max comes along in my life to teach me, something completely the opposite. While on our walks; there would be other dogs that would hang out with us, as we walked along the wooded property lines. One dog would pee on a tree; then another dog would pee on the same tree, just after the last dog did. Then Max would hop in there and pee on it to. Or sometimes, he would start the process. Sometimes a female dog would get in line, and try to pee on the tree like she was a male dog. *It was funny to watch.*

At first; I thought they were all trying to tell the other dog it was their territory, so back off. And or say they are the dominate leader of the group…

NOPE. Sometimes they would do a second round and by the third round; they were out of pee, but still trying to pee. It was cute and commendable at the same time.

BUT. In The Second Round I was noticing Max was smiling and wagging his tail. He was happy. Then I watched the other dogs more closely. They were all wagging their tails hard and smiling. Like they were all happy to see each other. And was saying hi to each other; at the same time, by peeing together on the same tree. *IT Blew my mind.* There was **not one** thought, of trying to be the dominate one of the group. This was my first live experience that creation *is not* territorial. There might be that one Self-Centered Love part of the Spirit creature, stalking others for prey. But that .01%? doesn't mean, all creatures are territorial.

Share His Treats and Toys with the squirrels. After our All IN Happy to See You, Dances were done. I went to grab a stash of Max's treats for him; while he decided if he was going to share, one of his toys with the squirrels. *Boom. Out the door.*

The first time Max shared one of his treats with the squirrels, I thought wait a minute. That's your treat for you… NOT to share with the animals. I picked it up to give back to Max. And Max would take and lay it back down, on the ground where I picked it up. *He looked at me.* OV; you gave it to Me and I'm choosing, to share it with the squirrels. With a just *trust me* on this one, look in his eyes…

Wow. That was powerful and I got goose bumps at the same time. We did our daily walk. We went back inside and was working on cooking, something for us. I sat down at the dining room table, looking out the porch sliding door window with Max. Both our eyes got excited. Looking at what Max was looking at. We both saw a squirrel coming down the tree; grab Max's treat and took it back up, to the first big tree branch to sit on. While sitting, it started to eat Max's treat. We looked at each other, and Max had that look on his face like… **SEE BRO!**

I was blown away; on how Max knew exactly what he was doing and he was showing me, that we can freely connect with creation. That's how I got started grabbing Max's Treats for him. I would give him one at a time; and Max would find that special place to put it, on our daily walks in the small woods next to our home. As soon as Max laid it down; he would look at me with his mouth open to grab the next treat, I handed to him.

This was one of the many things Max would show me; on how we can connect with creation, together as a family. Even after Max transitioned on; I would still lay a couple of Max's favorite treats by the first tree, that he first taught me at.

Max knew When I was Getting Upset with Something; he would put his head in my arm pit between my body and arm, to flip me over on my back. Then laid on my belly, with his full body weight. All in one swift movement. I would try to avoid or get out of it each time; but he knew exactly how to pin me down, to cool me off. It was like Max was the Coolest, Gentlest All Time *Grand Master* of Wrestling. I would lay in that position, for a few minutes and try to sincerely cool off. Max wouldn't get off me; *until he knew,* I was completely relaxed and peaceful. **Priceless**. The level of Unconditional Love Max has for those he loves, impressive.

Max Felt Bad Peeing and Pooping on the Floor. Max was so muscley; loved being outside and being with creation. That I was overly concerned; that *if anyone let him outside* when I wasn't home, Max would take off. And they wouldn't be strong enough, to go get him and bring him back. So I had him stay in the basement, when I was away from home. No matter how many times I told Max it's OK. It's not your fault. I don't expect you; to hold your pee and poop all day, when I'm gone. I will clean it up and **NOT** be mad. I would smile. And when I was done; give him hugs and rubs, until he was smiling again. Work day after work day, it would be the same routine.

Broke Out of a Room Made Out of Storage Totes. That's how he got his middle name. Max was getting bigger. Putting animals in cages is a no no to me. So; I took my totes of belongings and stacked them three high, in the corner of basement to make a nice size room for Max. He could walk around versus being squeezed in a small space, waiting for me to come home. Made it big enough as well; so that if he had to take a poop, he could do so off to one side. I went in the room made out of totes with Max. Sat down on his bed and relaxingly petted Max. While briefing Max, on why we need to make this work. *He looked at me like, sure.* So; I went outside the room for a brief minute, to see how he would do on his own. I comforted him and reassured him, this is better than being locked in a cage for 10hrs. Morning came, Max did his deed outside and into the tote walled room Max went. I gave him a long hug. It was always tough to say goodbye to Max.

Ten hours didn't go fast enough, but I was home and wondering how Max did. Max was at the door, greeting me with **ALL SMILES**.

MAX! What? I had to go to the basement to see how Max got out. Him being muscley, squeezed his way through a crack in the tote wall. *Hmm.* Re-strategized.

Got home the next day. Same thing. Max greeted me at the door with bigger smiles. *All I could do was smile back at him,* while we're doing our happy dancing. I went with a tougher tote wall strategy. This will do it.

Got home next day 2.0. And Yup. Max is **all** smiles, dancing and free. I was like. **NO WAY**. So, after we did our outside walk. I had to find out, exactly how Max is always finding a way to get out. So, I said Max show me how you are escaping, the tote walled room? I put him in there and waited on the other side, off to the side. Max didn't waste any time. Max was wiggling his body through, any crack he could. And boom, he was out again. All happy and excited to be back together. *All I could do was laugh.* And say, *Houdini you.*

Your middle name from now on will be Houdini. Maximus

Houdini Koan. We took all the totes down; and stacked them off to the side, where they came from. Went to the store and bought a gate for toddlers, and put it at the top of the basement stairs. This worked out better for Max's long days, while he was waiting for me to get home. This option gave Max the whole basement to hang out in. He and I felt so much better, he had more space to roam around. When my elderly dad moved in with me, I moved my bedroom down in the basement. Now Max was even happier; having a big whole bed to lay on, and knowing that's the bed we sleep on at night too.

Max Helped Me Write; Can My Life Change, President's Apocalypse, Gravity and Motion, Hell and Back, *and the Pinacol* (Epic Non-Stop Epiphanies) in writing this one; *Eternalizing Creation final phase.* **Priceless 100.0+**

The Top Three Were; One: After a long day and coming home to see Max greeting me; at the door as it opened. We always broke out *our* **ALL-IN** *happy dances.* **Two:** Going on our walks, and looking to play with the squirrels. **And Three:** Bedtime. Max would roll on his back and I would rub his belly. *ALL Priceless.*

At times; I still break down and cry from all those, emotional and physical memorable moments. We have shared in the past, as friends. It's been just over two years now; since Max has transitioned on. I still break down and cry… That's the impact of Max's Unconditional Love friendship, we had for each other.

Epic Best of the Bestest Friends Ever!!!

Beyond Epic. *My furry Friend! Thank you for assisting me while transitioning from; being a single parent to moving on, in pursuing my passions. My maturing as an adult, would have been completely different without you.* Your timing was all **too** impressive. Just the timing on waking up in the morning: to going outside; to taking breaks, etc. were mind blowing experiences. We would have otherwise not experienced, if the timing was just a few minutes either way. You put a smile on my face, every time I think about it. ***Thank You Maximus Houdini Koan for Bringing Us ALL Together, with Your Transitioning!***

NOTES: Why did I go to length in this tribute to Max, Cooper, Smug and Betsy? The more examples I could share of them; the more we can see the depth, of their Unconditional Love.

My furry friends; played an instrumental role in opening my eyes, to REAL examples of untainted Unconditional Love in motion.

Their true Unconditional Love for me; opened my eyes to what REAL Unconditional Love is, in a currently dominate Self-Centered Love controlled world.

REFLECTION MOMENT:

When I started to write this book;
it felt good holding this pen and writing
these words on these blank pages,
for the first time.
After the first few sentences;
I stopped and realized
I haven't composed a new book
since my dad transition on, a few years ago...
I must finally be at peace with my life.
(*a sober teary eye moment*)
I Know Enough to Want to Start this
New Journey Now, in Saving Creation from
Destroying Itself – Again.
... By Embracing this
Honor and Privilege with Max;
In writing this Final Phase
that Eternalizes Creation.
And Leading Us Through It,
with the Unconditional Love
part of the Spirit.

OV 2.0

2ND DEDICATION TO:

This Revelation is Dedicated to
All of Creation
That Choose to Let Go of
All of the Self-Centered Spirit part of the Spirit
That is within Them.
So that
They Can One Hundred Percent Plus:
Absorb, Embrace and Enrichen
Their External Existence With all of Creation.
To the Point:
Their Senses are 100% Restored and
Unconditional Love Manifests in All,
With All, Through All, Around All
And Beyond All

Forevermore!

Physically Eternal.

Wooooo Hooooo!

Congratulations!
We Did It All Together.

OV

Unconditional Love is Appreciated the Most
When it is Lost.

Why is That?

PREFACE

Warning&Disclaimer: This story may; and or will un-brain wash all the fragmented twisted truths, that the Self-Centered Love part of Spirit created. In hopes of burying the truth; and increasing the odds, it will never be discovered. This includes all of the stories, depicted by various "religious" artifacts. Yup. The Self-Centered Love part of Spirit is driven to destroy everything; that the Unconditional Love part of the Spirit created into existence, *so it can be at peace by itself again.*

Everyone has abstract time lines. No matter how long or short they are; in describing the possible origins of the past, present and future of creation. When done explaining, they are all still unknown and evasive. Even with the various "religious" artifacts' references. That allude to an eternal "righteous" tranny, with creation just vegetating as observers and accountable to a hierarchy. **No closed loops.** A lot of back peddling on their thesis. Which requires even more faith to believe in.

This is a confident defined time line. Start to Finish; with no rabbit trails of endless loops, of hopelessness and despair.

First; it's an honor and privilege to being one of the first in pioneering, this Final Phase of Eternalizing All of Creation. And at awe of physically sitting amongst the first– in the midst of – seeing the past; experiencing the present, while the future is consistently before us – in the now…

Waiting in anticipation for our very next moves; with the Unconditional Love part of the Spirit, in the beginning of this Final Phase. It will never exist again, nor will it ever be experienced again. We ALL will be so absorbed in living the now, in the eternalized physical state of existence. Immersed and saturated in Unconditional Love; in everyone and everywhere, all the time. Period. No clocks; no goals, no worries and at total peace living 100+% in the now. There will be no past, no present, no future. Just an ETERNAL NOW.

The urgency to write this book was first random thoughts here and there. I had Questions. Then Epiphanies would show up at the right moments. Like they were calculated answers; being spoken from the Core of the Unconditional Love part of the Spirit, with Max giving me soft intro ques. They evolved into monthly, then weekly to daily...

Now I sit here writing this book and I can't write it fast enough; for the urgency, to be at peace. While knowing in my heart that the Unconditional Love part of the Spirit is excited; to be interacting with us at a deeper enriching level, with all of its created creation friends on a grand scale.

This is what the Unconditional Love part of the Spirit has been compassionately waiting for; ever since it started creating all of Its created friend thoughts, into existence...

Like a Good Parent, patiently waiting for their child to want to take their first step on their own. **When they want to and when their ready to.** Both the parent(s) and the child enjoying, sharing that special enriching surreal moment together. **So, it is with this.**

I've had a good ritual routine growing up as a child on a farm within the "christian" faith, later in messianic judaism, Do It Yourselfer, Single Parent raising my three children by myself thirteen plus years, youth leader, shipping and receiving supervisor thirty-five plus years, fill in Plant Manager for three months and penning a few self-help books. Then to take a time out from all that, to stand back and absorb it all. Enough to be able to write this all down, even in a more balanced way. Versus if I didn't personally experience all those hands-on experiences.

Saying all that, now to move forward with what I'm about to write...

The "Creator" is a Spirit that is 50% Unconditional Love and 50% Self-Centered Love.

"God" the "Creator" is not a father, son and holy spirit Combo. Yup I said it.

A father, son and holy spirit concept; while throwing in the mix of a "fallen" angel called "lucifer" or the "devil", creates in the human mindset – fear. A list of must dos; I need to do to get to "heaven", the "devil" made me do it and portraying untold billions of ignorant humans being deceived.

All Those concepts, put all of mankind under a hierarchy. That hierarchy brain washing of understanding; leaves mankind only to hoping that "god" will forgive them by faith, to let them enter into heaven. If not, they are forever tormented in a "lake of fire." **Scare tactics 101**, by the deception and illusion the Self-Centered Love part of the Spirit created.

And or if they can reincarnate in different forms enough times; to attain a form of "immortal holy godliness," that sets them free from the reincarnation process. *Or worse yet*; everything is eternal, but when the body dies, the soul returns in a different *form/creature...* **This diminishes** the individual's *first unique created form*; from the beginning to the end, in becoming uniquely physically eternal.

The Spirit was by itself for eons and eons. *The Spirit is Endless.* The Spirit is Depthless. Nothing exists outside the Spirit. The Spirit understands all. If anything; eternally physically or spiritually exists and seems apart from the Spirit, it is because the Spirit created it into existence. Period.

The Unconditional Love part of the Spirit desires to: nurture and to be friends in, with, through, around and beyond anything that it has thought of – and created into existence. Even to itself.

Over eons of time; the Self-Centered Love part of the Spirit doesn't want any type of friendships, of growing together. It only wants to enjoy itself and with nothing else. Period. It's totally at peace with that.

This wore on the Unconditional Love part of the Spirit. It thought consistently about creating into existence new friends, but the Self-Centered Love part didn't want nothing to do with it.

Then the Unconditional Love part of the Spirit decided; that it was going to create into existence new friends, without the Self-Centered Love part of the Spirit's consent.

After absorbing that possibility; it decided to actually follow through and commit to it, **until the end.** The end is in reference to eternalizing all of which would be created; from the Unconditional Love part of the Spirit's thoughts, into the *individual's creature: spirit, mind, physical existence.*

Note: The Unconditional Love part of the Spirit first Created **ALL** Creation as Unique Spirits. That Individual Creation in spirit form; has real life and interacted/s with the Unconditional Love part of the Spirit, and the Rest of Creation.

In doing so; the Unconditional Love part of the Spirit ***realized*** that it was stronger, than the Self-Centered Part of the Spirit. That in itself; for first time experiencing that thought, ***produced a refreshing feeling*** to the Unconditional Love Spirit part of the Spirit. A feeling that it NEVER felt before, ever. Similar to Dopamine Rush Sensations; but at an Infinite Multi Depth levels, for the Unconditional Love part of the Spirit.

These first time **ever** dopamine sensations; were confirmations to the Unconditional Love part of the Spirit, to continue creating. The more the Unconditional Love part of the Spirit created; the more it confirmed to the Unconditional Love part of the Spirit, that creating was good to do.

Meanwhile as the Unconditional Love part of the Spirit continued creating. The Self-Centered Love part of the Spirit was being contracted; to make more room for this new creation, to be eternally part of the Spirit. The Unconditional Love part of the Spirit, felt more at peace than it has ever before. This too was refreshing and starting to become addicting.

The Self-Centered Love part of the Spirit began to feel restricted, cramped up. Its movement was starting to be restrictive. It was a weird feeling, that it has never felt before. Period. It was an "eye" opening experience, that the Self-Centered Spirit was hoping it would pass and never be felt again…

And this is where
**the Eternalizing Creation Final Phase
Revelation Begins!**

Unconditional Love is Appreciated the Most
When it is Lost.

Why is That?

IN THE BEGINNING BEFORE ANYTHING

PHASE ONE

When you base a story on time, events and places, it becomes impersonal to the point it loses validity.

When you base a story on never ending endless loops; of random learning experiences in trying to "ascend," it becomes disheartening for the masses while just a few "feel" like they've "ascended." Let alone, it diminishes the value of the unique individual creature and all of creation at large.

When a journey is based on emotionally connecting, it personally becomes an enriching life relationship. When one's passion is wanting to manifest it with all of creation; to become a part of the whole journey, it makes one's life journey even more enriching…

The only way we can truly connect emotionally is understanding what Unconditional and Self-Centered Love really are. Then make the choice for either side.

All other narratives are self-centered, distant and cold.

PHASE ONE THEME:
CHILD MINDSET AND DEVELOPMENT.

If the Unconditional Love part of the Spirit is infinitely wise; infinitely all-knowing of the beginning, present and the future.

But lives 100% in the now: infinitely eternal, infinitely self-sustaining, and has infinite Unconditional Love before anything was created. **Then** the Unconditional Love part of the Spirit can create eternal creation as friends; that are in Its likeness in spirit, mind, and in body. To the point; it's one seamless process that endures without any fear, of needing to make any deviations. Due to giving Its creation, the independent ability to choose.

Since all of creation was created in the likeness of the Unconditional Love part of the Spirit, then everything in creation is its unique version of Unconditional Love. Unconditional Love is infinite, so there's infinite amounts of unique creation examples of Unconditional Love. Humans are NOT the grandest form of them all. Humans are in equal standing; because we are all uniquely an example in creature/creation form, of the Unconditional Love part of the Spirit. NOT one likeness of Unconditional Love is greater than the other. The trees, soil, water, air, etc. and humans are the same. All in the likeness of Unconditional Love.

All of these created thoughts of creation, were all in spirit form first. Examples: the trees, plants, soil, water, air, creatures, humans, planets, etc.

The Unconditional Love part of the Spirit and all of the created thoughts of creation, were ALL talking to each other. All Enjoying each other's company/friendships. This went on for what seemed like eons, but all of it was still in the now. The Unconditional Love part of the Spirit was at total peace, more than ever. Unconditional Love part of the Spirit was truly pleased in its decision, to make room for its new friends. All unique and individually at peace as well. *So much so*; the Unconditional Love part of the Spirit NEVER wanted to go back at being lonely, ever again. Period.

This angered the Self-Centered Love part of the Spirit. This thought of being temporarily restricted, was just a weird feeling at first. But now with talks of being like this eternally, made the Self-Centered Love part of the Spirit – pissed off. NO WAY AM I GOING TO BE RESTRICTED, FOR EONS AND BE OK WITH THIS?

The Unconditional Love part of the Spirit was enjoying so much; in having all of these unique friends, that it ignored the feelings and thoughts of the Self-Centered Love part of the Spirit.

The Unconditional Love part of the Spirit was using words/communication, that the created thoughts couldn't understand. Observing all of these individual uniquely created thoughts, responses of *huhs*? – what do you mean?

The Unconditional Love part of the Spirit thought; I need to create physical sensations for them, so they'll be able to relate to me in a deeper way...

These physical sensations will need to be balanced and relatable; to create this deeper understanding, of what I am saying to them. This too will be refreshing to experience, with all of my uniquely individual created thoughts. Plus deepen their relationships with each other. **These sensations that they feel; will give them the same feelings, I had when speaking them into existence**...

Plus, the sensations I had when making room for them to exist. These will make our friendship with each other, even-more-deeper and enriching.

I will need to add to their sight and hearing sensations: smell, taste and touch. **Touch will be the greatest** *of all their sensations.* With all of these sensations; they will be able to understand everything to its fullest, with complete satisfaction in having our eternal friendship together and with each other. Forever and ever.

Unconditional Love part of the Spirit was having a deeper peace than it has ever had; up to this point of speaking its thoughts, into created thoughts.

Unconditional Love part of the Spirit rested in these thoughts for a while. But the more; the Unconditional Love part of the Spirit was engaging in it's new uniquely created thoughts. The more the created thoughts were becoming perplexed, without knowing why they were perplexed.

It was becoming more obvious than ever. But there was no rush to resolve this instantly. This is all a New Refreshing Created Experience; for the Unconditional Love part of the Spirit to Experience, and was enjoying it 100+%.

With the occasional checkups with its Self-Centered part of the Spirit; the Unconditional Love part of the Spirit was convinced this was the best decision it ever made, and was more committed to seeing it through. Until All would be at peace, understanding all, experiencing all in All their friendships and relationships.

This went on for quite a while, at a good relaxing pace. No rush. Even though everyone didn't completely understand what the Unconditional Love part of the Spirit was saying at times; they were getting really comfortable, in taking this new friendship experience with each other in baby steps.

Once the Unconditional Love part of the Spirit could feel; all of the created thoughts were relaxed and enjoying their baby steps, of enriching friendships together and with Unconditional Love part of the Spirit. The Unconditional Love part of the Spirit knew it was time, to introduce the three other sensations.

Unconditional Love part of the Spirit said, "Now that we are all comfortable with ourselves and everyone around us. Would you all be interested in going on a journey together?" All of the created thoughts were excited, but wondering what this new word *"journey"* meant. Then some of the created thoughts, spoke out loud and asked, "What is this word **journey** mean?" The *Unconditional Love part of the **Spirit's being*** had new tingling sensations, it never felt before. Plus; the asking of what this word journey meant, was in a relaxed manner. Versus all the previous times of being perplexed; confirmed to the Unconditional Love part of the Spirit that it was time to take these created thoughts, to *their next level* of awareness.

Unconditional Love part of the Spirit, was silent and *smiled.*

ETERNALIZING CREATION FINAL PHASE

The Created thoughts; was wondering what the Unconditional Love part of the Spirit was thinking, behind its smile. Then they smiled back. *All were **at peace** in the moment.*

Up until this time; the Self-Centered Love part of the Spirit was getting somewhat contented, in getting use to being cramped up. But now it was starting to feel concerned, with what the Unconditional Love part of the Spirit was thinking about … going to *"**this next level.**"* …

Why can't the Unconditional Love part of the Spirit be contented, with what it has already created? It's already taking my space. It's going to take more? It feels like the Unconditional Love part of the Spirit, has MORE Self-Centered Love than I do?

The Unconditional Love part of the Spirit ignored the Self-Centered Love part of the Spirit; and kept gently moving forward in baby steps, with its newly created thoughts.

The smile peacefully vanished into saying … "**JOURNEY!**" This word is like going on a Creating Making Adventure together. It's like how I created all of you, but now we All will be creating together.

All the featureless faces on all the created thoughts, ***quickly turned into smiles*** then ***busted out*** *in excitement. A sensation they* never felt before. It was so strong that the Unconditional Love part of the Spirit, felt it too.

The Unconditional Love part of the Spirit was so proud of the created thoughts, learning and experiencing this on their own and enjoying it. Plus; this confirmed to the Unconditional Love part of the Spirit, it was moving at the right pace with the created thoughts.

To the amazement to the Unconditional Love part of the Spirit, all of the created thoughts said together – in their own way – **When can we start?** *What can we do?*

Unconditional Love part of the Spirit was **soaking** all that enthusiasm into its Core. These first-time, never felt before sensations were priceless. "We can more than *surely* start now."

All of the created thoughts busted out with even more enthusiasm.

"BUT." Said Unconditional Love part of the Spirit.

All of the created thoughts went straight to silence. What was this word ***BUT?*** By now all of created thoughts were getting use to hearing new words, they never heard before and didn't understand.

Unconditional Love part of the Spirit went on to say, "We all need to go over and observe the Self-Centered Love part of the Spirit now."

All of the created thoughts turned their sights to looking and observing, the Self-Centered Love part of the Spirit. But shortly afterwards, they wanted to move away from looking and observing.

Unconditional Love part of the Spirit said, **"Watch More.** See how and what, the Self-Centered Love part of the Spirit is doing."

The created thoughts were showing signs; they didn't want to anymore and just moved their sights, away from the area of the Self-Centered Love part of the Spirit.

Unconditional Love part of the Spirit said; "When we go on this Creating Making Adventure together, we will be looking just like how you saw the Self-Centered Love part of the Spirit doing."

All of the created thoughts *went silent again.*

Unconditional Love part of the Spirit continued; "Even though you will be looking like what the Self-Centered Love part of the Spirit is doing now, from time to time. You will get three more sensations; that will allow you to understand every word I say from now on, and throughout all of eternity. These three sensations are: Smell, Taste and Touch…

Touch will be *the Greatest Sensation that we will ever create in All of Creation.* **Period.** Touch will speak more words than you can ever say and mean, *throughout all eternity together.* Touch will allow you to see things; that your eyes can't see, at the moment. Touch will give you ideas of what something might taste and smell like. Touch will allow you to show the depthness; of your Unconditional Love in your friendships and relationships, in the deepest possible ways…

Touch will allow you to maximize your spirit, mind and body; to the most enriching experiences you will ever have, throughout all eternity…

Touch will give you the same awareness of the sensations; I get in creating and going on this friendship journey, with you all and throughout all eternity."

All of the created thoughts were all in; in giving the Unconditional Love part of the Spirit, their attention to everything the Unconditional Love was saying.

All of creation was extremely curious.

This too was sensations, that Unconditional Love part of the Spirit and created thoughts had never felt before. PLUS, both were now; more than ever convinced, to going on this Creating Making Adventure together.

After a moment of savoring this enriching moment with all of the created thoughts, Unconditional Love part of the Spirit continued. "What makes this Creating Making Adventure together even more satisfying is; we will all be in the same like mind sharing our individual experiences together, in complete harmony with each other for all eternity…

AND… this Touch Sensation will be continually taking our journey, to the next level throughout ALL Eternity. ***Together***."

All of the created thoughts are lighting up like a million+ suns, listening to every word the Unconditional Love part of the Spirit is saying. Then…

"**BUT!**" Unconditional Love part of the Spirit said in a louder tone than ever before.

The created thoughts excitement instantly dissipated. A sensation that ALL of them never had before.

Silence... *More silence.*

The Unconditional Love part of the Spirit continued slowly in a soft compassionate firm tone..." Once we start this journey, we can't stop. This journey will be as long as you want and need it to be. **You will determine** *the length and time of the journey."* Silence.

More silence. "Look closely at the Self-Centered Love part of the Spirit, in how it's moving around. It's sadness. **Never forget that. Never** while we are on this Creating Making Adventure together. **NEVER!**" Silence.

All of the created thoughts are still, all attentively listening.

More silence. "What you see here, will get worse and worse. *Imagine* ... what the Self-Centered Love part of the Spirit is doing now, with what space it has. Imagine if that space gets smaller and smaller."

Silence... "Now... How would you personally think – if I never created you. All those conversations we had together never existed? Would you be sad like the Self-Centered Love part of the Spirit is now?"

"Remember when you were a thought before I created you? Remember how you felt when you went from a thought to being a created thought?"

The created thoughts were somewhat understanding what the Unconditional Love part of the Spirit was saying. While starting to show signs of sadness; thinking about never having all those conversations, with the Unconditional Love part of the Spirit. Now in a fragmented way; they were starting to understand how the Self-Centered Love part of the Spirit was feeling, but in the opposite way.

The Unconditional Love part of the Spirit gave them some good time, to absorb those thoughts. Then continued, "Remember these thoughts and never forget them!" "These thoughts will help us all get through this Creating Making Adventure together, and to the other side of it."

Silence... "Then we will NEVER EVER lack anything; in our friendships and relationships together, throughout all of eternity. TOGETHER! PHYSICALLY SPIRITUALLY ETERNAL. FOREVER AND EVER!"

All of the created thoughts spirits *were more excited then ever before.* Even though they all didn't completely grasp, what the Unconditional Love part of the Spirit was saying. They were now getting stoked, about this Creating Making Adventure together.

They all have now accumulated enough enriching moments; with the Unconditional Love part of the Spirit, to fully trust the Unconditional Love part of the Spirit. To the point; the Unconditional Love part of the Spirit could feel 100+% of the sincerity and commitment, that all of the created thoughts had. Individually and All together. They were All in one mindset and spirit.

PLUS PLUS now getting stoked on being All in One - in this new physical body they were all getting.

They were ALL in AWE of this Surreal Moment they just experienced together. It was too a sensation they never had before.

Silence sets in. The silence continued for some time. This silence was like the silence they all felt before, when the Unconditional Love part of the Spirit spoke them into created thoughts. This time however, they are all building on that last sensation. Which deepen their Unconditional Love for themselves and with each other. All of created thoughts were completely appreciating and understanding; the understanding of growing in baby steps.

This growing process makes it more meaningful and rememberable; from the beginning, through it and throughout all eternity.

The Unconditional Love part of the Spirit was proud of itself for being patient and compassionate; with all of the created thoughts in their growing process, in becoming individuals and in their friendships. This too was a new sensation, that the Unconditional Love part of the Spirit never felt before. And confirmed even more to the Unconditional Love part of the Spirit; it's decision in wanting to create friends to be with, throughout all of eternity. **Plus,** this is the best decision *it ever made.*

More silence. Truly epical. The knowing that everything that they experienced up until now, will never be the same again. Never. So, they all were savoring this enriching moment with Unconditional Love part of the Spirit **EVEN MORE**. To the point, everyone was contented in not saying nothing at all. If they did, they only did it with their eyes.

It went on like this longer, to the point the Self-Centered Love part of the Spirit begin to believe... maybe all of these created thoughts that the Unconditional Love part of the Spirit, were gone! *Dude that would be so cool.*

The Self-Centered Love part of the Spirit began to think; it had a bad dream and now was awakening, to having all of its space back. The Self-Centered Love part of the Spirit got up and looked around. *NOPE. THEIR still here.* But they are All silent. **Why?** The Unconditional Love part of the Spirit is silent as well. **Why?**

The Self-Centered Love part of the Spirit asked the Unconditional Love part of the Spirit, "*Why are you ALL silent?*" Silence lingered.

The Unconditional Love part of the Spirit said with a peaceful soft tone, "*you know why... I want friends*"

The Self-Centered Love part of the Spirit **looked at the Core** of the Unconditional Love part of the Spirit. Then said, "If you follow through on YOUR Intentions, then You will have to choose between Me or THEM... **Period!"**

The Unconditional Love part of the Spirit, *sadden.*

They both had never felt these sensations before. NEVER. **EVER.**

The Unconditional Love part of the Spirit... ***deeply looking at the intensity*** *of all of the created thoughts; listening and getting excited about their Creating Making Adventure together, with the Unconditional Love part of the Spirit...*
was convinced NOW more than ever; that it too was going to have to go through, some uncomfortable deciding moments as well.

Everyone was in complete silence now. Relishing the moment, the decision they were ALL about to make. **NOTHING** ever was going to be the same, after this decision... **PERIOD...**

Do they all go forward in this NEW journey?

Or does Unconditional Love part of the Spirit let go of all its created thoughts as friends, and return to being alone with the Self-Centered Love part of the Spirit?...

Returning to the Total Spirit, of being Eternally Peaceful with itself once again.

The Silence NOW SUPERCEDES All of the Silences before.

All of the created thoughts are quietly, patiently waiting on the Unconditional Love part of the Spirit's decision. Even though they haven't felt real pain. Now they know more than ever, this Journey may or may not happen. And they all will have to be contented in going back, as just being thoughts. While knowing what they know now, with the Unconditional Love part of the Spirit.

This page intentionally left blank.
To Allow *that* Moment to Resonate deep within our
Spirits, Minds and Bodies...
to connect with it once again.

The Unconditional Love part of the Spirit when at the right moment of oneness, said to all the spirits of created thoughts…

Let's Embark on This Journey Together?!

UNANIMOUSLY all of the spirits of created thoughts, shouted **YES!!!** with their whole beings.

That one huge impact defining moment of connecting core to core with the Unconditional Love part of the Spirit; still resonates consciously and sub-consciously in the CORES of all creation it created, throughout all the phases of eternalizing creation. PERIOD… *from that day forth and forever will be…*

To the point… At any time someone says; let's embark on this journey together, the excitement synergy is heightened. The more it's said from the core, the more compounding effect it has on all of creation. Especially in the restoring ALL of our senses; to one hundred percent plus as they were in the beginning, when first physically created.

The Unconditional Love part of the Spirit then turned; and looked at the core of the Self-Centered Love part of the Spirt, knowing it was stronger than the Self-Centered Love part of the Spirit …

In one quick decision, without the Self-Centered Love part of the Spirit knowing it. And or phantoming it; the Unconditional Love part of the Spirit, contained the Self-Centered Love part of the Spirit into one location. This one location was pure Self-

Centered love. There was zero trace of Unconditional Love in it...

*This one location is called the **Abyss**.* In recent Self-Centered Love part of the Spirit creating tradition, it is referred to as the "Tree of Good and Evil." ***A better title is*** The Home of 100% Pure Self-Centered Love. The door to its home is in the same shape of a living tree. And there is a window in the door.

Side note: It's funny to think that something Self-Centered in nature, could even think about or do something good for creation.

The Self-Centered Love part of the Spirit felt portrayed, by Unconditional Love part of the Spirit. It was all at the same time infinitely: panicking, angry, revengeful, anxiety and depressed...

The Self-Centered Love part of the Spirit; was getting more and more uncomfortable and frustrated, as it was being forcibly contained into one area. Once it hit tipping point; the Self-Centered Love part of the Spirit relaxed and was feeling more at peace being by itself, with no one around. **Aaah.**

Yup, peaceful. Because it was the first time in what felt like a long time; that the Self-Centered Love Spirit didn't hear any thoughts of created creation, speaking and interacting with the Unconditional Love part of the Spirit. It took being at peace, over being cramped up into one "tiny" location.

The Unconditional Love part of the Spirit did not want the Self-Centered Love part of the Spirit, to influence any of the Speaking Creation into Physical Existence.

Silence...

The Unconditional Love part of the Spirit, looked at ALL of the spirits of the created thoughts. "When would you like to born into physical creation?"

They were looking at the Unconditional Love part of the Spirit with excited perplexity on their faces...

"You can be the first of all physically created or wait later as to the phase you want to be a part of, and when during that phase."
...

They continued to listen.

"You can choose to be with your friends and companions, to make your journey more enriching." After the Unconditional Love part of the Spirit said this...

Their perplexity dissipated completely into being 100+% excited.

The Unconditional Love part of the Spirit proceeded to go through all the five phases of their Creative Making Journey, they were going through together. So that all of creation would understand fully; all the words that Unconditional Love part of the Spirit was using, to describe experiences...

"The child phase, the adult phase, the friend phase, the companion phase and then the parenting phase...

Each phase will give you a deeper understanding of these words, from a different experience perspective. Once you complete all five phases, you will understand the complete meaning of these words forever. And We will ALL be forever peaceful, and contented in all of our enriching relationships with each other."
...

The Unconditional Love part of the Spirit. Stops. And watches their enthusiasm heighten.

All of creation started talking with their friends and companions, in what phase they wanted to be in. The more they got involved, the more they became confident in their decisions.

The Unconditional Love part of the Spirit continued, "You can only pick one phase; phase two through phase five...

And be physically created once. You are you and no one else. This is your/our unique Creative Making Journey together...

It doesn't matter what phase you pick; you will personally experience all five phases of being a child, adult, friend, companion and parent when your physically created." The Unconditional Love part of the Spirit stops...

Noticing ALL of creation tuned out the Unconditional Love part of the Spirit. All of created thoughts were 100% all in; with their planning when to be physically created, with their friends and companions.

Unconditional Love part of the Spirit, was smiling big time. At peace like no other. Enjoying and savoring each one of these baby steps, they are taking together. No rush. **Totally** in the NOW.

Another confirmation to the Unconditional Love part of the Spirit, it made the right decision in creating physically eternal friends.

Once they all pretty well had their chosen phase; they quieted down and turned their attention back, on the Unconditional Love part of the Spirit. They were ALL smiling at each other and getting more and more excited, about their Creating Making Journey together.

A common question was starting to emerge in the curiosity of ALL creation, "How are we going to be physically made?"

The Unconditional Love part of the Spirit was patiently and compassionately waiting, for this moment to come. The best time to teach, is when everyone wants to sincerely know how. This means they are ready to learn; and want to apply what they are learning, immediately... "When I first thought of you ALL, I made male and female versions of each type of creation...

This way, when the male and female want to create a child together, they can participate in the physically creating creation process."

They were all listening intently. BUT had that perplexity feeling, starting to show up on their faces.

"I will gently take your created spirit and put you into your new created physical body. Slowly. Allowing your spirit to become one with your physical body and with your mind." The Unconditional Love part of the Spirit paused…

They were all still listening intently, as their perplexity turned into HUH?

"Ok. Let's put it this way. When I say it's time to jump into your physical body. You jump in it; like you're jumping into the water, to go swimming! Does that make more sense?" The Unconditional Love part of the Spirit was using an experience they loved doing.

They ALL Lite Up like a million + suns, **"Yeah!"**

Everyone went into complete silence again. They were all mastering and enjoying taking this journey in baby steps. Savoring every moment. One moment is as great as the last and no one moment is greater than the other.

"BUT."

All of creation was getting more used to hearing, the Unconditional Love part of the Spirit's soft intros. In describing how they will be feeling, looking like how the Self-Centered Love part of the Spirit was being cramped up… so the Unconditional Love part of the Spirit's core was using, a more sobering tone this time.

This got their attention to listen deeper.

"Pending on which part of the phase two through phase five you choose to become physical created, you might not remember who you are and where you came from." Silence…

"Example. Your senses are at 10 and your memory is at 10. When you jump into your physical body, your senses and memory might go down to 1 or 2. Making it really hard/uncomfortable to navigate through the physical world." …

"To help you make a better decision on which phase you want to get your physical body in, I will explain it in terms of 1 through 10. The number 1 will feel like, how you saw the Self-Centered

ETERNALIZING CREATION FINAL PHASE

Love part of the Spirit is cramped up in its abyss. The number 10 will feel like you do here in the now, and like jumping in the water to go swimming."

As the Unconditional Love part of the Spirit was describing the number 1. The created thoughts were soberly showing on their faces, them thinking about the Self-Centered Love part on the Spirit cramped up in its abyss. When they heard about the number 10, they all lite up like a million + suns.

The Unconditional Love part of the Spirit could see that they were engaged, in the conversation and wanting to learn more. In hopes they could reference back to this moment, while in their physical body.

The Unconditional Love part of the Spirit continued, "All During Phase Two, your numbers will be at 10...

During the first part of Phase Three your numbers will be at 9. As we go through this Phase, your Numbers will trend down to 1."
...

When All of creation heard the number 1, their eyes got as big as they could. **Like holy bananas wide.**

"During the first part of Phase Four your numbers will be at 1. As we go through this Phase your Numbers will trend up to 9. And at the End of the Final Phase your Numbers will All be on 10...

"All During Phase Five your numbers will be at 10 forever."

Silence...

The Unconditional Love part of the Spirit was so enjoying this moment; while seeing all of created core's thoughts, were All in at trying to absorb this Creative Making Journey process together.

"This will be the core framework; to hold each phase together and to be uniquely appreciated, along this journey. *One phase will not be greater than the other.* Each phase is required...

Each Phase will be even more appreciated in Phase Five." Silence ...

"All Five Phases are required to Learn and Lock in the Meaning; and Depthness of these five words: Faith, Perseverance, Compassion, Forgiveness and Peace. Forever!" ...

The Conditional Love part of the Spirit was going to take a break. BUT saw how intently ALL of the created thoughts, were hungry to hear more and continued...

"Now... even though the number ranges, in the Third and Fourth Phases will be trending down then up. At any time during these phases, the meaning of these words can be completely understood and applied. Understanding and Applying the meaning of these words to one's journey, will speed up the restoration of your numbers to 10...

"Example. One created thought might understand the meaning of these words and applying them in Phase Three. If their number was trending down; then their number stops trending down and can start trending up. While those around them, continue to trend down...

"And the same in the Fourth Phase. One created thought might understand the meaning of these words, and applying them in Phase Four. If their number is trending up, it will trend up faster...

Silence.

"As your numbers trend upward, this is a part of the restoration process of your senses...

"When your senses are trending downward; it will get harder to see, listen, taste, smell, touch and understand. When your senses are trending upward; it will get easier to see, listen, taste, smell, touch and understand...

"When your numbers are trending downward, your sensitivity towards each other will get lesser - distant. When your numbers are trending upward, your sensitivity for each other will get greater – closer...

"When your numbers drop to 8-9 you will start to lose sight

of ALL OF US. When your numbers are 1-7 you will not see us at all. You will and or will start to doubt everything, you have experience prior...

"When your numbers trend back up to 8-9 you will start to see all of us. When your numbers return to 10, you will see everything as it was, is and will be."

SILENCE ...

All of the created thoughts absorbed all of these analogies in. 100%. Their faces showed their appreciation for the Unconditional Love part of the Spirit; using the numbers 1 through 10, to describe what they would be feeling during these Phases. They knew 1 + 1 = 2, 2 + 1 = 3, etc. They commonly used numbers in their conversations already...

More Silence...

Now with this added understanding they started tuning out again. Due to them honing in to which Phase they wanted; to be FOR SURE physically born in, with their friends and companions...

They were all in; and connecting at a whole new deeper level, which brought them closer in this Creative Making Journey together.

The Unconditional Love part of the Spirit was smiling big time. **Enjoying** every moment of it. Listening to their individual reasons, why they wanted a particular phase. Pros and Cons, etc. ...

It was priceless seeing everyone 100+% ALL IN, in their Creative Making Journey together.

Those who were super stoke chose to be in Phase Two. Those who were half as stoked chose to be in Phase Three. Those who were driven to understand, chose to be in Phase Four. And those who were relaxed, sit back and enjoy chose Phase Five...

The Unconditional Love part of the Spirit thought, that was fascinating. That All of the created thoughts basically choose the Phases; in the sequence to when the Unconditional Love part of the Spirit, first thought of them as thoughts...

It was like that sequence, was ingrained into their nature and personality.

Example. Those creation that the Unconditional Love part of the Spirit thought of first wanted to go first, those second wanted to go second, etc. and those towards the end want to go last...

Now the "end" doesn't reference to being all done. This "end" reference is to when the Unconditional Love part of the Spirit; decided to speak it's thought friends, into created thoughts.

Another way of saying this is, it thought friends were in the Core of the Unconditional Love part of the Spirit. When the Unconditional Love part of the Spirit spoke them into created thoughts, the created thoughts were "birthed" outside its Core. The created thoughts could freely move around; in the Unconditional Love part of the Spirit, as independent unique spirits.

As they were getting close to the end; of those deciding which Phase to be in, there was those who *seemed indecisive*. They wanted to be in each of the Phases. It was hard for them to choose...

The Unconditional Love part of the Spirit was picking up on this and said, "All of us on this side of those choosing to be physically created; will be able to see them and interact with them "spiritually" and pending what number they are on, will be able to hear and see us. If not; some will be able to sense with their premonitions, when we are trying to get their attention and or want to connect with them...

"We can also study and be apart of a Phase; observing indirectly and take that knowledge into the Phase, we are going to be physical made...

"Example. If we want to be a part of Phase Four; we can

ETERNALIZING CREATION FINAL PHASE

observe in great detail Phase Two and Phase Three and take that knowledge with us into Phase Four, when we are physically born into it...

"Keep in your mind; that those observation experiences can make such a huge impact on your sensations, that your core will be convinced you were physical born in each of the Phases. Even though you've only been physically created one time, in one Phase only...

"The observation knowledge that you obtain will make you stand out from the rest; as "having" great knowledge and awareness of the "greater" view, of ALL of creation."

Silence...

"Now if you are observing *your now* physical friends in their Phase; and if they are in a higher number range like 8-9, they might be able to see and interact with you...

"If not; they will highly be able to sense your present with their spirit, and interact with you at that level. They might need tests to verify if it is you. *Examples:* Have an object moved to a location, that it normally isn't at...

"Or the timing of pieces of information, you can hear what they are thinking. *Make it happen for them* and they'll know without a shadow of doubt, it is you. Because they did not physically tell anyone. This will get them excited like no other, that they are actually communicating with you."

MORE Silence...

All of creation was now feeling more comfortable and confident in their decisions, in which Phase they wanted to become physically created in...

All of creation had their choices peacefully and excitedly locked in, except for one last group. Especially now knowing they can be in contact, with their friends in different Phases...

This group was really contented skipping these Phases Two through Four. Watching and observing all of others; being physically created before them, and **Totally-*being*** at peace with it...

The Unconditional Love part of the Spirit wasn't at all surprised, at how they were appearing to be disengaged. These were the friend thoughts, that were created long after the first friend thoughts were. The Unconditional Love part of the Spirit was getting so use to; and being at peace with creating infinite amounts, of endless friend thoughts into existence ...

The silence was longer than normal. This got ALL of creation's attention. They ALL were now looking at the Core, of the Unconditional Love part of the Spirit...

The Unconditional Love part of the Spirit was smiling. But this time the smile was more of a smirk...

This took All of creation by surprised, and they had this curious look on their faces...

The Unconditional Love part of the Spirit then giggled, in reaction to their curious looks on their faces...

They were all waiting for the Unconditional Love part of the Spirit, to explain its smirk and giggling responses...

The Unconditional Love part of the Spirit stopped giggling, and never told them what it was thinking *at the time...*

Between me and you; the Unconditional Love part of the Spirit was realizing and enjoying ***it was*** Addicted to the Infinite Amount of Adrenaline Rushes, it was getting while creating infinite amounts of friends.

Yup. Throughout ALL OF ETERNITY.

The Unconditional Love part of the Spirit continued; "Remember these sensations of excitement and oneness, you are experiencing with each other right now. And how you have been interacting with your friends and companions. Embed these sensations deep into your cores, right now." …

ALL of creation quieted themselves down. And went through all the great memories that they had individually, with their friends and with their companions. Then embedded them deep in their cores…

Everyone was thoroughly enjoying; their memories and joys, they had experienced up until this moment. Enjoying all those baby steps they took together; to make their experiences that more enriching, with each other. Even including this moment. TOGETHER. It will never be the same again, once the first created thoughts are physically created. **NEVER EVER AGAIN…**

They relished this moment so much; they did this routine several times…

Each time they did; the more they realized how much they deeply loved each other and the Unconditional Love part of the Spirit, for giving them this opportunity to become eternal physical friends…

As they were getting close to being done, with embedding their sensations experiences with each other and this knowledge. They could feel that long silence, in waiting for the Unconditional Love part of the Spirit's decision…

Was it wanting to return back; to being one with the Self-Centered Love part of the Spirit, as the Spirit? Or proceeding forward, in creating them as eternal physical friends?

The **Unconditional Love part of the Spirit broke** the silence with; "Your embedded sensations in your cores; will guide you to your friends and companions, when you wake up in your physically created bodies…

All of Creation gave the Unconditional Love part of the Spirit a big **HUH?**

The Unconditional Love part of the Spirit said, "Close your eyes like this."

They All did.

The Unconditional Love part of the Spirit peeked to see, if they were all closing their eyes. **Yup.** The Unconditional Love part of the Spirit is loving every baby step they are taking together, to make this and every experience they have more enriching...

"Now open your eyes!" ...

They All did.

The Unconditional Love part of the Spirit said, "This is what I was referring to... when you wake up in your physical bodies. When you wake up in your physical body; *its going to feel like* when you went from a thought, to a created thought. It's going to be the same sensation, but way bigger. Depending what number; you are at in the Phase, you might feel confused... like those perplexing moments you have from time to time...

During these moments your embedded sensations in your cores; will guide through your Phase, to find your friends and companions...

Silence...

"When you get close to finding your friends; your embedded sensations in your core will give you signs and sensations, that they must be one of your forever friends. As you connect more with your physical created friend, the more your core embedded sensations will verify it. You and your friend will click, at whatever you do together. This to will verify to you, that you found one of your forever friends...

"This goes for the same when you find your companions. The sensations embedded in your cores will be firing on all cylinders, to the point you will feel like you are "soulmates." A word you'll hear others say. But for you it will be "spiritmates." ...

ETERNALIZING CREATION FINAL PHASE

"It might take you a long time to find your spiritmates. When you do, you might not have very much time together. But when you do, it will make your spirits soar..."

"You will be able to find your friends and companions a lot faster and easier, if you can choose to be physically created as close as you can to them."

Silence...

All of creation was now fine tuning their decisions with their friends and companions; to where and when they wanted to be physically created in their Phase of choice, during their Creative Making Journey Together.

Once done, they all quieted down to Silence.

More Silence...

They all have been in this moment several times before. **And every time** it gets better and better, more enriching than the last time. To the point of enjoying every one of these baby steps, *are getting addictive...*

This time though, they all know what's going to happen next. So... they enjoyed these last few moments ALL together, looking deeply into each other's eyes... thinking about all the physical experiences, they about to enjoy with each other...

The Unconditional Love part of the Spirit gave them a lot longer time, to embed this moment deep into their cores.

The next time All of creation is going to be experiencing this same moment; but in their eternal physical bodies, is going to be at the beginning of Phase Five.

"One more last thing to embed into your cores is the sounds of music. Embed them deeply within your cores, your favorite musical sounds. If and when you feel perplexed; because you can't find your friends and companions, after being physically created...

When you hear those sounds; those sounds will activate your physical sensations, to help you find your friends and companions." The Unconditional Love part of the Spirit said in a *soft firm* tone...

They ALL busted out in *humming* their favorite musical sounds.

Once their humming music sounds started to resonate within the Unconditional Love part of the Spirit, it began to cry...

It was all the musical sounds the Unconditional Love part of the Spirit was making, when it was infinitely speaking them ALL into created thoughts...

The Surreal Humming Sounds could be heard everywhere...

Unconditional Love is Appreciated the Most
When it is Lost.

Why is That?

CREATION SPOKEN INTO PHYSICAL EXISTENCE

PHASE TWO

When you base a story on time, events and places, it becomes impersonal to the point it loses validity.

When you base a story on never ending endless loops; of random learning experiences in trying to "ascend," it becomes disheartening for the masses while just a few "feel" like they've "ascended." Let alone, it diminishes the value of the unique individual creature and all of creation at large.

When a journey is based on emotionally connecting, it personally becomes an enriching life relationship. When one's passion is wanting to manifest it with all of creation; to become a part of the whole journey, it makes one's life journey even more enriching...

The only way we can truly connect emotionally is understanding what Unconditional and Self-Centered Love really are. Then make the choice for either side.

All other narratives are self-centered, distant and cold.

PHASE TWO THEME:
ADULT MINDSET AND DEVELOPMENT.

After everything bursted into perfect physical existence; the Unconditional Love part of the Spirit and All of Creation, "stood" in awe of each other. They were all in their baby forms and fully conscious in the *"garden"* called Earth. Starting out in baby form was to give all of creation; all the same experiences in the beginning, of their physical existence.

Out of all of the creation that Unconditional Love created, **the greatest was touch**. Without the touch sensations; creations physical presents would not be any different, from its spirit only presence. Unconditional Love created physical touch; so that the created spirits of creation could feel the depthness of their Unconditional Love for each other, and with Unconditional Love part of the Spirit.

AND... The Main Reason *Why* the Unconditional Love part of the Spirit created touch; was to give the created spirit creation the same sensation experiences, that Unconditional Love part of the Spirit felt. When it first thought of creating friends to interact with, for the first time.

Speaking all of Unconditional Love part of the Spirit's created thoughts into physical bodies; **touched the core** of Unconditional Love part of the Spirit, *to its Core*.

Again; the Unconditional Love part of the Spirit discovered it was *way stronger* than the Self-Centered Love part of the Spirit, when it was physically creating the spirits of creation. The Self-Centered Love part of the Spirit didn't resist; even though it was frustrated, by being extremely uncomfortable.

Earth was the starting point; for all of the Unconditional Love part of the Spirit's thoughts of created spirits, to be physically manifested. This made the connection with all of the spirits of created thoughts closer, to being complete with the Unconditional Love part of the Spirit. After that first moment; of being physically spoken into existence was thoroughly enjoyed, by all creation and the Unconditional Love part of the Spirit...

The Unconditional Love part of the Spirit would create other "earths" throughout; what appears to be an infinite continually expanding "universe," within the Unconditional Love part of the Spirit.

The Unconditional Love part of the Spirit is everywhere; connecting and inter-connecting with each individual creation, core to core in the NOW. AND ALL THE SAME TIME with: Creatures, Plants, Different types of Dirt, Water, Air, Etc. None is greater than the other. All are the same living creation, in the likeness of the Unconditional Love part of the Spirit.

Why all creation started out in baby form? The Unconditional Love part of the Spirit loves All of the Created thought creation so much; that the Unconditional part of the Spirit wanted all of physically created thought creation, experience the same experiences. So; no one felt left out and couldn't relate, to what the other creation were talking about. When being a baby formed in the womb of their mothers, and growing up as a child into an adult.

Plus. Plus. They could ALL relate to their offspring, at a deeper subconscious level. Their parental bond with their offspring would now be at 100% plus. This sets up a strong foundation for the first physically created thought parents, to not be dumb founded at raising and nurturing their offspring. They could easily relate.

As the first created spirits being physically created as babies, were moving around interacting with each other verbally. The Self-Centered Love part of the Spirit could hear their voices and noises, outside Its Abyss door.

The Self-Centered Love part of the Spirit's total peace and quiet, was annoyingly abrupted again. This turned the Self-Centered Love part of the Spirit's frustration; into hatred towards the physically created thoughts, that were just physically created as babies. But it couldn't do nothing about it. ***It was physically restricted into one location.*** In the Self-Centered Love part of the Spirit's Core; this was a non-stop nightmare, that continually got worse every minute. A few times; the Self-Centered Love part of the Spirit would look out it's door window, and see the little babies crawling around making noises. Then growing up as children making noises, and then as adults making noises...

Every time there after; the Self-Centered part of the Spirit would despise the babies, that were being physically created...

It regrets that it was weak, against the Unconditional Love part of the Spirit from the beginning. When the Unconditional Love part of the Spirit first had the thoughts of having eternal friends. If only it was stronger than the Unconditional Love part of the Spirit, then ***none of this torment*** would be happening now.

As the first male and female humans were becoming young adults; some of the conversations they were having with the Unconditional Love part of the Spirit, sounded to them like mumbo jumbo. Some of the words they still didn't understand. No matter how many examples the Unconditional Love part of the Spirit showed them, they still remained clueless of what the words meant. Towards the end of all these examples, they were still yearning to want to know...

Now in their physical bodies they were more-hungrier than ever; to engage in a more deeper enriching relationship, with the Unconditional Love part of the Spirit...

Finally; they asked, "What must we do to understand ALL these words: Faith, Perseverance, Compassion, Forgiveness and Peace?"

(All the words the Unconditional Love part of the Spirit would use to describe the sensations and feelings; it was experiencing when creating them as thoughts. Then into created spiritual thoughts, then into physical created spiritual thoughts).

Due to being created eternal and "perfect" in the beginning (not any of that in a trial creation basis, test and the retry non-sense) Unconditional Love part of the Spirit is Perfect and Eternal upfront – not over time.

Note: It's the Self-Centered Love part of the Spirit that needs to test and retry.

Unconditional Love said, The Permanent Fix to this and for all the generations proceeding you; is to Release the Self-Centered part of the Spirit, into all creation... *There was a heaviness that came upon the Unconditional Love part of the Spirit, after saying that.*

Note: The Unconditional Love part of the Spirit wants and desires a two-way relationship and friendship with All of Creation. **BUT at physical creation's speed,** of wanting to connect with Unconditional Love part of the Spirit. Nothing is rushed in real relationships. Both are taking one baby step at a time; in their new friendship relationship, as being physically created. So that both are enjoying it at the same pace. In the same spirit, mind, and body phases.

Note: This process, makes the Unconditional Love part of the Spirit and Physically Created Thought Creation in the same core set: in spirit, mind and body. In their friendship relationships with the Unconditional Love part of the Spirit, as Eternal Friends. Not a "Lording Over You" non-sense narrative; we've been brain washed to believe, by the Self-Centered Love part of the Spirit.

The first male and female humans said, "Why are you behaving like this? This is new to us. We thought we knew you."

Unconditional Love part of the Spirit said, "Because I know the pain you and all of creation will suffer."

They said together, "What is this Suffer?"

Note: The first male and female humans were in one spirit, mind and body; with their untainted Unconditional Love relationship, they had for each other. *One was NOT "Lord or Over" the other.* Both where physically created at the same time as babies. **Yup.** This gives them the same experiences to be able to relate with each other; at the deepest levels of who they are, throughout their entire relationship. Forever.

The Unconditional Love part of the Spirit continued, "I will show you everything; only if you're going to commit to going to the end, to obtain this understanding."

They said, "WE WILL!" Because they were deeply yearning to understand fully; what the Unconditional Love part of the Spirit was telling them, in all of their conversations from the beginning. For the core purpose; of having a more enriching experience with the Unconditional Love part of the Spirit, as eternal ALL IN friends. *Versus being tag-a-longs*. They wanted to be all in with their relationship with Unconditional Love part of the Spirit. Eternally. They truly loved the Unconditional Love part of the Spirit, with ALL OF THEIR CORES.

"**Wait.** You have no idea what you are saying. Saying and DOING are two different things. Saying it without the experience is completely different, than actually doing it with the experience," the Unconditional Love part of the Spirit said in a *soft firm* tone.

They remembered that *tone* before, and quieted themselves. But this time; it was the first time in their physically created bodies, and their new sensations were firing on all cylinders.

Silence. Savoring this baby step moment together; the

Unconditional Love part of the Spirit continued, "Let us go and see together what I mean, by all of physical creation will suffer."

The first male and female humans; lead the way over to the tree door of the abyss, of the Self-Centered Love part of the Spirit. And looked into the tree door window of the abyss, to see the suffering. They quickly became so heavy, that they turned away. *"What is all this?* Why are we feeling this way? This is all new to us," the first male and female humans said almost in unison.

Note: The things they were seeing were all of the things; that the Self-Centered Love part of the Spirit *wants to do* to all of the created thought creation, that were created by the Unconditional Love part of the Spirit. *In Doing*, so that all of the thought created creation would *become non-existent*. And the Self-Centered Love part of the Spirit would be by itself, and return to its infinite space of peace once again.

Note: They were seeing all of the generations of the future; being destroyed by all types of ways, illusions and with short life spans. All of these insights were in one fast big blur; with some stop points in between, showing horrific scenes of creation being brutality ripped to shreds. Mass murders; lush lands becoming waste lands scorched within minutes, and with near extinctions of all physical creation sprinkled in between.

"This is what death and separation is. You loose most of your senses. You become cold, confused and lonely" said the Unconditional Love part of the Spirit in a *soft sobering* tone.

They said, **"WHAT IS ALL THAT?"** The first male and female humans were more confused than ever, especially due to all of their new added sensations in their bodies

A short moment of silence. "These are all the things; I experienced when I separated my Self-Centered Love part of my Spirit from my Unconditional Love part of my Spirit, to make room for you to exist." ...

"Remember? It was the most horrible thing I did, to put my Self-Centered Love feelings aside." ... **silence**...

"But as I created more and more thoughts of friends; I started to feel refreshed, more alive than ever before. I GOT EXTREMELY EXCITED; that I was going to have infinite amounts of generational friends forever, versus living all by myself forever and ever with the Self-Centered Love part of the Spirit." **Silence...**

"All because I didn't want to inconvenience, my Self-Centered Love part of my Spirit?" Silence...

"The more I thought about it; *it didn't make sense* to being ok with loneliness, like the Self-Centered Love part of the Spirit does. So, I made the decision to commit to the end... I became aware of: Faith, Perseverance, Compassion, Forgiveness and Peace *even more* coming into existence; as a result of the process in physically manifesting, my thought created creations...

The Unconditional Love part of the Spirit was enjoying thoroughly every minute, of their friendships growing deeper and deeper.

They said, "Let us ponder about this more. Then we'll give you a decision on making this commitment; to wanting to understand these words you've been talking about, so that we can be more like you."

The first male and female humans felt peaceful, in their decision to wait. They were applying; their learning on how to take baby steps, in their enriching friendship relationships. **Plus;** this gave them time to absorb and understand, all these new sensations they were feeling in the process.

Time past.

The Unconditional Love part of the Spirit asked the first male and female humans, "Are you sure you want to learn about these words together?"

They said, "We have thought about the commitment of wanting to know; and the sacrifice of all of physical creation would have to go through, just for us to know what these words mean…

At first; it felt like what you referenced to earlier about letting go of the Self-Centered Love part of the Spirit, to create us and all of creation as friends. Are we being what you say, "Self-Centered" too? … Making all of creation suffer; because we want to know the meaning of these words, to be just like you?" …

"But then as we thought about it deeper. We came to the conclusion; if we don't commit now, then later some other generation does…

"We won't still have that understanding, even though the rest of creation after that point will. So; to be the accountable first male and female humans, we must make this decision to commit to do it now." …

"You have been so kind to us with your Unconditional Love towards us; to start us out as babies when you first physically created us, from being created thoughts. That gave us the understanding of how and what our children will go through. In their process of being woven together in the first female humans; to birth, to toddler and now becoming young children themselves." …

"It is our responsibility to commit to going through this process…

"While we are experiencing that process; of making room in our lives for the children, that we will be having. In doing so; we can now relate to how you were feeling, when you were creating thoughts of us into existence." …

"If that helps us to become more in your Unconditional Love part of the Spirit likeness… **And in this knowing;** we will be doing this commitment with you, while we're "losing" all of our senses. *It now becomes a must*, that we do this now." …

"We now believe with and in all of our core beings; that by going through this too, this will make us completely like you. In truly knowing what these words mean; because we experienced them just like you did, but from our perspective." …

"Then we can all become physically eternal with all of creation. Together. Forever. Never ever having to go through that again; and or at a later generation wanting to, if we don't do this now… That in itself; would seem to make the process dragged out even longer, than what it needs to be…

"Because we want to be "*Selfish*"? Nope." …

"With all that said; moving forward we want the reassurance that we will be able to get through this commitment, and onto the other side of it. We would like to go again, to the tree door of the abyss of the Self-Centered Love part of the Spirit…

"And look in the window with you. To look for someone in a future generation; that will be the catalyst, to ending the cycles of destruction to creation… If we can find someone then this will be a sign to us; that we did and have learned the meaning of these words, you speak about so frequently but we don't understand." …

Silence. More silence. The male and female humans along with the Unconditional Love part of the Spirit was savoring these new awarenesses together; for the first time as friends, in this Physical Creating Making Journey together.

Unconditional Love part of the Spirit was at total peace and excited at the same time; that the first male and female humans had reasoned this, on their very own…

This made the Unconditional Love part of the Spirit even happier; that it made this decision to follow through on physically creating thoughts, of all kinds of creation friends. And ignored the Self-Centered Love part of the Spirit.

The Unconditional Love part of the Spirit knew without a shadow of doubt; that they were having a two-way accountable responsible relationship, with the physically created thoughts creation. This new feeling of awareness in physically created creation; gave the Unconditional Love part of the Spirit a whole new infinite level of sensations, it never ever felt before. It would be like what you call a dopamine rush. Times infinity.

"OK. Let's go to the window of the tree door to the Abyss." Unconditional Love part of the Spirit said in a *soberingly soft* tone.

As they were All moving towards the door of the Abyss. There was more sober excitement then they had last time. This was too a new sensation they all shared together, for the first time. It deepened their Unconditional Love for each other even more.

They All quieted themselves down. Looking deep into each other's cores.

More Silence…

Then gave each other that look, they are ready…

This time looking into the window of the tree door to the abyss; they looked past all the destruction that the Self-Centered Love part of the Spirit was creating, to destroy all of the physically created creation. Generation after generation. Some times they were close in finding someone, that fit their requirements to commitment. *But none availed…*

They still pressed forward in looking, at the next generation then onto the next generation. This made them more determined to find someone. Due to the need in looking harder for someone. They realized even more; that this had to be the only way to justify, making this commitment decision NOW. Period...

The more they looked; the more they saw how more determined the Self-Centered Love part of the Spirit, was in destroying all of creation.

When the Self-Centered Love part of the Spirit had to deal with another generation to eradicate, the more angier the Self-Centered Love part of the Spirit got. It went from *soft deceptive intros* to deceiving the masses, to full blown aggressive slaughters.

It went to great lengths to develop *"religions"* to justify the killing of babies and children; to gain more human *"powers"* of control. But that wasn't enough. It tried cutting down the life spans of creation. That wasn't enough.

The will and determination in creation; in wanting to connect with the Unconditional Love part of the Spirit grew stronger and stronger, due to the intensifying annelation of all of creation.

Until one human appeared in the future; showing signs of wanting to connect, with their inner self. The Where and Whys. Along with a deeper observation of all of creation; wanting to connect with Unconditional Love part of the Spirit, in their own special ways with caution...

The more this human observed Unconditional Love part of the Spirit; and what was being said about a *"Creator"* of all this creation, or how creation came into existence. And THE hows in all these come full circle, to entering an eternal peace...

They both didn't connect in meaning. Something was being distorted, to the point nothing connects. Everything being said; was hypothetical and had to be accepted by faith, with no other options of outcomes…

This appeared to drive this human; into a deeper understanding, of what the Unconditional Love part of the Spirit really is. And if it is this; then this has to be true as well. True Unconditional Love is patient, kind and steadfast; in wanting a two-way friendship versus a one-way relationship…

Then what appeared to be happening with this human; he was having epiphanies, one after the other. Confirming that this human was truly making connections, with the Unconditional Love part of the Spirit…

"Is this what we've been looking for? Is this our future reassurance? We need in making this decision and commitment; to the understanding of these words, the Unconditional Love part of the Spirit is always referring to?" … this is what both the male and female humans were thinking and communicating, to each other without saying a word.

Note: This is common and normal, when all of physical creation's senses are 100+% active. Or when their Core Number are on 9s and 10s.

They stopped looking through the tree door window to the abyss; and they looked at each other, into each other's eyes. They both got excited together. Like a baby realizing for the first time; it can walk on its own, versus crawl. This too made their friendship with the Unconditional Love part of the Spirit, even more enriching than before. With themselves and the relationship they had for each other…

This time though, they gently hugged each other. Then their eyes did the talking ... just like the Unconditional Love part of the Spirit said about; how the physical touch sensations will say more than all the words, can say together... **They smiled.**

Silence set in for a moment, as they all savored it together.

They turned back and continued to look in the window of the tree door of the abyss. They all wanted to subconsciously look into the eyes of the human; that was seeing and understanding these insights, from their future. *Then at the right moment*; they saw that human stop what he was doing, and looked right into their eyes...

At first, they were all taken by surprise. They wanted to look into that human's eyes, but wasn't expecting the human to be aware of them looking at him. *Is this another sign?* They were thinking to themselves...

Then immediately after they had those thoughts, it was like that human knew what they were thinking. And that human said to them with his words, "**YES. *I will complete the process of this commitment, in wanting to know the meaning of these words.* **So that all of creation can be set free; from the destruction the Self-Centered Love part of the Spirit wants to do, in removing from existence - all of creation. So that the Self-Centered Love part of the Spirit can go back to enjoying; all of Its infinite space by itself, like in the beginning.*"

The words that came from the mouth of this human; while looking into their eyes, made them speechless...

The thoughts that they had as the first male and female humans with Unconditional Love part of the Spirit; in following through in putting this commitment in motion, **was just verified** from a future generation...

They had successively satisfied their core's desire; in making sure they were all at peace, in making this decision. This confirmed in their cores; that this process of physically eternalizing creation was in the CORES of all humans, from the beginning and throughout all eternity...

It was a decision a human had to make. Because the first male and female humans was the last thoughts of created creation; that the Unconditional Love part of the Spirit had, when creating all of creation as friends.

After they all enjoyed that experience. Even with that human from the future being subconsciously there with them, *enjoyed it with them as well.*

Then they all became silent.

Then the first male and female humans asked Unconditional Love part of the Spirit, **"What must we do next?"**

"You sure?" said the Unconditional Love part of the Spirit.

"YES, WE ARE!" they said... *Silence...*

Unconditional Love part of the Spirit said, "You know *saying* is totally different from *doing*?"

"**Yup**. We know. And now we are ready to embrace this commitment; with all of our cores and beings, because we have seen the end results of our decision. *All of creation;* will know the meaning of these words you freely speak about, even though we don't understand them now. We as well with all of creation, will now know. None will be void of this understanding. None will be left out, in enjoying a total awareness of all of your experiences. So that they can relate with you in every way; enjoying a complete and the fullness of an Unconditional Love relationship and friendship with you. **FOREVER**"

The first male and female humans were in total one core agreement, in saying this to the Unconditional Love part of the Spirit. Without blinking an eye. Without stuttering. And without hesitation.

The way their words were being conveyed, from the cores of the first male and female humans. The Unconditional Love part of the Spirit knew they were ready to commit to this decision, in wanting to know the meaning of these words. Plus was ***extremely*** pleased and satisfied; with the first male and female humans coming to this conclusion together, by themselves...

The Unconditional Love part of the Spirit was getting more ALL-TIME high sensations; from making its decision, to physically create the created friend thoughts into existence...

This too, was the first time ***they all*** had experience this emotion. All were elated by it; on how it was making their relationship with each other, more enriching than before.

Meanwhile *as this was going on with them; that human was still looking at them and subconsciously listening, to their verbal and mental conversations they were having...*

Then the first male and female humans said together, "What must we do to start this process?"

Unconditional Love part of the Spirit hesitantly said slowly, knowing what it was going to have to deal with. But was more excited about physical created creation; wanting to have this deeper understanding, so that they could have a deeper more enriching friendship relationship with Unconditional Love part of the Spirit. That made the Unconditional Love part of the Spirit's core; feel even more ecstatic about the decision it made in proceeding to create friends. Plus; enjoyed all the new tingling sensations, while thinking about all these thoughts...

*Then **cautiously** said,* "You must open the tree door of the abyss together; and let the Self-Centered Love part of the Spirit out, to go feely throughout all and into all of creation. So that All of Creation will understand these words." ...

The first male and female humans looked at each other in silence; then in silence together, looked at Unconditional Love part of the Spirit...

In the lingering silence; that human was still watching them and hearing everything, that was being said and or thought of.

Then they had this funny feeling that human was still looking at them, observing their conversations. This too; gave them the comfort and the feeling of being more confident, in making their decision to this commitment. Being connected with the whole process from beginning to end.

More silence. *More hesitation...*

That human picked up on this and said to them, "You open the tree door of the Abyss; to release the Self-Centered Love part of the Spirit out, to freely go anywhere in creation. *I will release* the Self-Centered Love part of the Spirit from all of creation; to return the abyss, to stay there until its decision day." While in an eye-to-eye contact; without breaking contact, while speaking in a soft compassionate tone of reassurance to them.

More silence.

More hesitation... But this time at awe, that the human was actually apart of their moment together. It felt like that human was physically there with them; even though he was from a future generation, but *it was the core* of his spirit, mind and body.

This too *was the final confirmation in their hearts*; that they were making the right decision together to this commitment, in wanting to understand. And be more like the Unconditional Love part of the Spirit, in sharing these same emotional experiences together.

These experiences would deepen their enriching relationship/friendship more than ever. Plus give all of creation that same understanding, so that they too can have that same Unconditional Love enriching relationship/friendship together.

More silence...

Then the first male and female humans said, "Let us enjoy being with our families and all of creation, for a few more days. We will let them know, the decision we have made and what to expect... Also, the understanding on what will happen and why it's happening. So that they too will be a part of this decision."

With that; the human that was observing them and being apart of the decision said, "I love you. Thank you for acknowledging, I was truly looking at you and being a part of this decision. It is an honor and privilege to be with you, in this Journey of Eternalizing Physically All of Creation. *Plus*, with this experience of understanding what true Unconditional Love is. From the Beginning and into all of Eternity. **PLUS PLUS Thank you** for verifying all the epiphanies and revelations, I been having about all of creation from the beginning to forever."

Silence. They were intently listening to that human with all their cores and beings. Getting tingling sensations as well.

The human from the future said in closing. "You won't need to look me up again. And or let me know the day you're going to release the Self-Centered Love part of the Spirit, out of the Its Abyss... By the time; it's my time to be physically created into the world, and been a part of it. It will be confirmed to me; that it did happen and it wasn't my imagination... *I love you and thank you tons!* ... Bye for now!"

As that human disappeared from the tree door window view, they looked at each other *in deeper awe* than before. They assumed that the human would be more shocked/surprised, then they would be in seeing him. They were impressed by the confidence; that the human had in knowing who he was, and who they were. *And the confidence* in knowing the whole process of Eternalizing Creation, more than they had…

Which in turn; produced a confidence in them that it was a decision, ***they had*** to make. And there was no other choice; in knowing and understanding the words the Unconditional Love part of the Spirit, freely talked about.

The Silence was more compelling than before. It was a silence that was peaceful versus the apprehensive feelings, that the first male and female humans were feeling before.

Then they said to Unconditional Love part of the Spirit, "**We SINCERELY Thank You**. For letting us make this decision commitment in baby steps. It was priceless! This too deepens our enriching relationship/friendship with you and with each other."

The Unconditional Love part of the Spirit was overwhelming enjoying their friendship relationship even more, at a deeper level. It was totally at awed; at what it created and had no second thoughts in doubting its decision, to physically create the thoughts of creation. And said, "**I LOVE YOU.**"

And for the very first time ever, the Unconditional Love part of the Spirit cried. *This too was refreshing.*

The first male and female humans were staring at the tears, that was coming from the Unconditional Love part of the Spirit's Core. "What are those flowing out from your core?"

"Those are tears. This is what happens when you Love someone Unconditionally and you want to enjoy it, without talking about it. This too is another form of communication."

They said, "Interesting...

From the looks on the faces were tears, that we saw in the window of the tree door to the Abyss. We wondered what they were, but was more interested in finding that human."

They all left the tree door of the Abyss and enjoyed their families; friends and all of creation, for the next few days. During their interaction with them, they would tell them about their decision and what it will do for all of creation...

They all took it the same way; as the first male and female humans took it, in the beginning. With that experience prior; the first male and female humans helped them understand, it in a deeper way...

Some excited; some not so excited, but all understood that it was the best thing to do for all of creation...

To do it now, versus another generation in the future making that decision. It would make this experience a longer process...

With that, all of creation was in agreement with the first male and female humans. No doubts. **All of creation was ALL IN**; to the point it was engrained into all of their CORES, like with the first male and female humans...

As the first male and female humans was seeing this; as they went throughout all of creation, they were becoming even more at peace in their decision...

Now they knew this was the right time; to proceed to releasing the Self-Centered Love part of the Spirit into all of creation, to start the next phase in this Physically Eternalizing All of

Creation Journey.

With that; the first male and female humans went back to their place of abode, and enjoyed a few days with themselves and their family.

All of physically created creation with the Unconditional Love part of the Spirit; were peacefully savoring all of these new sensations they were feeling, individually with their families and with all of physically created creation.

Once they enjoyed themselves; the first male and female humans said to Unconditional Love part of the Spirit, "We are now ready to release the Self-Centered Love part of the Spirit from its Abyss."

Unconditional Love part of the Spirit said again from its core, *"Are You Sure?"* ...

They both said together; **"WE ARE!"** The tone of their voices was in FULL Confidence, versus in the beginning when they were saying it.

Unconditional Love part of the Spirit noticed the difference in the tone of their voices. And replied, **"OK. Let's do it!"**

They were all confidently, going towards the tree door of the Abyss of the Self-Centered Love part of the Spirit.

Meanwhile; the Self-Centered Love part of the Spirit was listening ALL the time, during through this whole decision-making process...

By the looks on their faces, when looking through the window of the tree door to the Abyss...

To what that human was saying to the first male and female humans, from a future generation. The Self-Centered Love part of the Spirit **heard <u>EVERYTHING</u>** that human said. Their complete plan was exposed from the beginning, to the ending...

This made the Self-Centered Love part of the Spirit; even more determined to destroying all humans, by what ever means. First by killing all the babies it can, in hopes that it kills that future human in the process...

Then for cheap entertainment; the rest of creation, to the point nothing exists...

All of this information; put the Self-Centered Love part of the Spirit, into survival mode. It created updated new plans for future generations; that the first male and female humans wouldn't/didn't see, while looking in the window of the tree door to the Abyss...

For the first time, the Self-Centered Love part of the Spirit **was happy again.** It was game on time. The Self-Centered Love part of the Spirit, was all in and drooling...

The first male and female humans reached the tree door of the Abyss, looked at each other in peaceful silence. Then turned back around, and looked in the window of the tree door of the Abyss. **They were STARTLED.** They were looking into the face/Core of the Self-Centered Love part of the Spirit. And the Self-Centered Love part of the Spirit, was smiling back at them...

Well aware of what and why they were doing there. **And it wasn't another show and tell view day...**

It was D Day. Decision Day for **ALL** of creation...

The opening door knob on tree door to the Abyss, was designed to have two human hands open it. It had to be the hands of one male and one female human companions…

The door knob also could detect; if the male and the female humans was in agreement, to open it. If they were not, then the tree door would stay closed…

This was brilliantly made before hand, by the Unconditional Love part of the Spirit. This design ensured whoever opens the door; it could only be by the hands of a male and female couple, who cores are in agreement with the decision…

What's even more awesome; is the Unconditional Love part of the Spirit was gently waiting for creation, to make this decision on their own. When they were sincerely ready. ***Plus; even more ready***, *when they included All of Creation to make the decision together.*

The first male and female humans *slowly* put their hands on the **FREEZING COLD** tree door handle to the Abyss, while looking into the eyes/Core of Self-Centered Love part of the Spirit…

*This is the first time they ever felt "**cold**" with their touch…*

But the warmth of their Unconditional Love for each other, superseded the freezing cold door knob. They had full confidence in what and why they were doing…

The Unconditional Love part of the Spirit was thoroughly impressed and proud of them, at the same time. ***It never felt this experience before.*** It sent tingling sensations, throughout the Unconditional Love part of the Spirit's **whole** infinite being. This too was making ALL of their friendships and relationships journey together; that more enriching than ***EVER*** before…

While still looking at the Self-Centered Love part of the Spirit in the eyes; with full confidence, they turned the tree door knob to the Abyss to open it…

All of creation was apart of the experience, and ALL IN supporting it…

This too made Unconditional Love part of the Spirit be at awe and teary eyed. That All of Creation wanted to deepen their friendship and relationship; with Unconditional Love part of the Spirit, in a more enriching way - from their cores and total beings...

This confirmed even more; that this was a *sincere two-way relationship*. They All wanted to grow together baby step by baby step. **A Priceless Moment,** in *All of Their Friendship Creating Making Journey together.*

Just before the last movement that will allow the door to freely open; they looked into each other's eyes, then into the eyes of Self-Centered Love part of the Spirit one more time...

Knowing that ALL of creation was completely about to change, but didn't have a clue what that meant.

Then first male and female humans and all of creation took one last deep breath of PURE Unconditional Love; untainted by the Self-Centered Love part of the Spirit, for the last time...

Looked Self-Centered Love part of the Spirit in the eyes...

The Self-Centered Love part of the Spirit responded back with a *loud chilling scream of*, **YOU ARE ALL-DEAD NOW,** *feel to it.*

The first male and female humans stopped one last time. Turned around and looked silently at all of creation...

And All of Creation said with their body language, **LET'S DO THIS!**...

Looking at their faces; gave them that final confidence, the first male and female humans were doing the right thing. Knowing all of creation was behind them, through this whole Creating Making Journey.

The Unconditional Love part of the Spirit was at total peace *more* than ever; with its decision to physically create its friends' thoughts of created creation.

With that, the first male and female humans opened the tree door of the Abyss... sheer silence at epic proportions.

Even though the Self-Centered Love part of the Spirit was excited to be **free, it hesitated**...

It was finally going to be free, from all of that time of being restricted...

But now was doubting itself, for the first time. *EVER..*

All of creation was confidently looking, with their *Cores DIRECTLY* at Self-Centered Love part of the Spirit...

The Self-Centered part of the Spirit was thinking, What does All of Creation know, that I don't know? ...

Why is All of Creation willingly doing all this when they can live in "*paradise*" forever; without going through all this pain, I'm about to inflict on them? ...

Some more hesitation.

All of creation is witnessing together; the doubt Self-Centered Love part of the Spirit has, *but is covering it up with anger.*

This heightens all of creations relationships even more, with the Unconditional Love part of the Spirit.

This confirms with all of them; this is most defiantly, without a shadow doubt the right decision.

More hesitation...

All of Creation is now confidently peacefully smiling with all of their cores, at the Self-Centered Love part of the Spirit.

The Self-Centered Love part of the Spirit *is re-strategizing its plan to eliminate all of creation, once and for all… **thinking intently.***

Hmm… Aah…

If Unconditional Love part of the Spirit created all of this; **THEN WHAT CAN I CREATE TO COUNTER IT,** *that will assist me to speed this up and increase my odds of succeeding?…*

After pondering on how to incorporate this new thought; Self-Centered Love part of the Spirit, smiled back at all Creation with a ***new found confidence.***

All of Creation aware of the Self-Centered Love part of the Spirit's thoughts; ***smiled with even more confidence,*** back at Self-Centered Love part of the Spirit.

The Unconditional Love part of the Spirit was now having **COMPOUNDING** infinite amounts of tingling sensations. This once more was confirming its decision, to physically create its created thought friends…

While witnessing with All of Creation, that this was truly a two-way relationship. That the Unconditional Love part of the Spirit was seeking to have; with all of its infinitely created thought friends, throughout all of eternity.

ETERNALIZING CREATION FINAL PHASE

Unconditional Love is Appreciated the Most
When it is Lost.

Why is That?

CREATION LEARNING:

Faith, Perseverance, Compassion, Forgiveness and Peace.

PHASE THREE

When you base a story on time, events and places, it becomes impersonal to the point it loses validity.

When you base a story on never ending endless loops; of random learning experiences in trying to "ascend," it becomes disheartening for the masses while just a few "feel" like they've "ascended." Let alone, it diminishes the value of the unique individual creature and all of creation at large.

When a journey is based on emotionally connecting, it personally becomes an enriching life relationship. When one's passion is wanting to manifest it with all of creation; to become a part of the whole journey, it makes one's life journey even more enriching…

The only way we can truly connect emotionally is understanding what Unconditional and Self-Centered Love really are. Then make the choice for either side.

All other narratives are self-centered, distant and cold.

PHASE THREE THEME:
FRIEND MINDSET AND DEVELOPMENT.

When the Self-Centered Love part of the Spirit was released for the first time in all of creation; it had a lot of panic, anger, revenge, anxiety and depression. Sprinkled in all of that; was the new sensation it never felt before, the touching of creation…

A tad addictive, but only to destroy it.

The Self-Centered Love part of the Spirit totally relaxed; to think deeper on its strategy, to be more systemically. Versus going on random rampages, leaving loose ends here and there…

What was the quickest way to eliminate all of this creation? And convince the Unconditional Love part of the Spirit; it was a TOTAL MISTAKE and WASTE OF TIME, in making eternal physical friends…

PERIOD…

The Self-Centered Love part of the Spirit went back over and studied the pattern; the Unconditional Love part of the Spirit went on, to create its eternal created friends. **HMMM…**

First… Thoughts, **Second**… Created Thoughts, **Third**… Relationships with the Created Thoughts, **Fourth**… Teaching Created Thoughts and **Fifth**… Enjoying Eternity with Physical Created Thoughts.

These descriptions, were from the Self-Centered Love part of the Spirit's point of view.

"Now all I have to do is flip this backwards; and it will erase everything that the Unconditional Love part of the Spirit did, without any traces of the physically created thoughts. The Only thing left *will be the **deep scars;*** on the Unconditional Love part of the Spirit's Core, to remind the Unconditional Love part of the Spirit *to **NEVER** to do this again…*

"First… Thoughts. **Flip:** I will enter into their thoughts.

"Second… Created Thoughts. **Flip:** Create Doubts.

"Third… Relationships with the Created Thoughts. **Flip:** Condition them to Accepting Mental and Physical Abuse is ok.

"Fourth...Teaching Created Thoughts. **Flip:** Embed in their cores to Never trust anyone and anything. Everything is trying to destroy their lives. Paranoia at it's finest.

"And Fifth... Enjoying Eternal Created Physical Thoughts. **Flip:** Enjoying all of eternity with only Myself and the Unconditional Love part of the Spirit as **ONE SPIRIT**. AGAIN...

"Perfect. **I LOVE THIS STRATEGY.**" The Self-Centered Love part of the Spirit was thoroughly proud of its strategy. *Relaxed*. And had the biggest smile, then quickly turned into busting out laughing. It's laughing was so deep and satisfying, it permeated all of creation...

All of creation instantly felt a change in their cores, that they never felt before. All of their number 10s were vibrating and weaken.

The Self-Centered Love part of the Spirit could feel all of physical creation's cores weaken. This was giving the Self-Centered Love part of the Spirit adrenaline rushes, that it never felt before. And went quickly into Addiction Mode.

Even though, the Self-Centered Love part of the Spirit wanted to go full open season. It stopped. Relaxed and realized this was confirmation, that this strategy was going to work. HMM...

aaAh. *Almost forgot.* Since the Unconditional Love part of the Spirit can create, then I can create as well. This strengthened the Self-Centered Love part of the Spirit's in taking more time; to come up with an overall strategy to destroy all of creation, the first time versus random rampages...

Let's see. I need to create fear in creation, so that All of Creation will justify in destroying each other...

Ooooh... I need to create creatures; that will have no fear in destroying Unconditional Love part of the Spirit's creation, with no remorse. Like me; my creatures will get satisfaction and adrenaline rushes, from destroying them as well... *this is getting exciting!*

As the Self-Centered Love part of the Spirit was feeling these new sensations; it realized that the Unconditional part of the Spirit was feeling the same sensations, when making its creation.

Then a thought popped into the Self-Centered Love part of the Spirit's Core, maybe we are to create creation? It immediately went into **NO**. Thought leave my Core **NOW**. That's insane. NO PEACE. NO SILENCE.

NEVER ENTER MY CORE EVER AGAIN. The Self-Centered Love part of the Spirit. Went on a rampage.

This Mental Ramage was so deep, all of physical creation could feel it. Most of their vibrating 10s went to 9s. Some of them were starting to lose sight of their spiritual created friends, yet to be physically created. Their five sensations; sight, hearing, tasting, smelling and touching were being affected. The vibrant colors weren't so vibrant. The sounds weren't as detailed. The tastes weren't as distinguished. The smells weren't as sharp. And touch was becoming numb.

The Self-Centered Love part of the Spirit could feel the effects; of its first aggressive rampage, against physical creation. And it was digging it.

Physical creation all quieted themselves down. Looking at each other. Thinking maybe this wasn't a good idea; letting out the Self-Centered Love part of the Spirit, into all of creation?

The Self-Centered Love part of the Spirit smiled at the hearing of their thoughts. "I have successfully got into their thoughts. While instantly creating Doubt... *I'm on a roll, dude*. This is going to be too freaking easy. I'll be able to destroy all of creation, faster than the Unconditional Love part of the Spirit Created it...

Aaaah... Feeling that eternity peace and quiet already.

Aaaah... Aaaaaaaaaaaah!

Most of the creation, that ignored the Self-Centered Love part of the Spirit's mental rampage. The rampage didn't affect their cores, as it did with the humans...

During that experience, their cores at 10 were vibrating and temporarily went to 9s. But for the most part, they all went back to 10. This strengthened their ignoring the Self-Centered Love part of the Spirit...

The physical creation reactions; to this Self-Centered Love part of the Spirit's Mental Rampage, distinguished themselves apart from each other.

Example. The dog species created thoughts, were the first to be created thoughts of the Unconditional Love part of the Spirit. They had such a blast in hanging out with each other, the Unconditional Love part of the Spirit put creating on hold. This went on for some time. Both at peace being with each other, all the time. This experience created; a higher density of Unconditional Love into the cores, of the dog species. Thus; their undying sensitive Unconditional Love they have, for humans and all of creation...

As their having a blast hanging out with each other became "normal," Unconditional Love part of the Spirit proceeded to create more creation thoughts. With the dog species thoughts; right there beside the Core of the Unconditional Love part of the Spirit, as a faithful companion. Eager to be there; and a part of the Unconditional Love part of the Spirit's creating, new creation thoughts. Intermittently the dog species would start playing with the Unconditional Love part of the Spirit's Core; to get the Unconditional Love part of the Spirit attention, to take a break...

The Unconditional Love part of the Spirit would smile at the dog species, then go all in at playing together...

Then back to creating creation...

The dog species deeper density of love for the Unconditional Love part of the Spirit; is greater than all the other thoughts, that the Unconditional Love part of the Spirit created. This was like this in the beginning; and throughout all the phases, until Phase Five. In Phase Five; all of Creation will have the same 100% density of Unconditional Love for and with each other, as the dog species had in the beginning.

Note: The Pitbull type dog species was the first of the dog species to be created. Then later throughout the thought creating journey in the beginning; the Unconditional Love part of the Spirit would create more variety of dog species, to be friends for the Pitbull dog species...

◆ ◆ ◆

As the Unconditional Love part of the Spirit was getting caught up, in creating more and more thoughts of creation. It noticed that the Pitbull type dog species was sitting off to the side, and missing its playtimes with the Unconditional Love part of the Spirit. Thus the Unconditional Love part of the Spirit sensitive to this; created other types of dog species intermittently throughout, to keep the Pitbull type dog species engaged with the creating thoughts journey.

Every time the Unconditional Love part of the Spirit stopped creating thoughts; and created another type of dog species for the Pitbull, the Pitbull would start wagging it's tail like no other. Doing an **ALL IN** happy tail wagging dances, with the Unconditional Love part of the Spirit. **EVERYTIME.** Like it was the First Time.

Example: The rest of the creation; except for the humans, was the same as the dog species in their excitement, but NOT as noticeable to the humans...

When humans take the time through phases three through four; to gently and compassionately connect at a deeper level with the rest of creation, then creation will respond back with Unconditional Love as well.

Note: Those physical creation created by the Self-Centered Love part of the Spirit, will not respond back in Unconditional Love. This is how we can verify which creation; was created by the Self-Centered Love part of the Spirit, when our cores are below the number 10. At 10 and maybe some what of at 9; we will be able to clearly see everything as it is, without needing to subtle test first.

Example: The first male and female humans along with the others; were created towards the end of the Unconditional Love part of the Spirit's creating thought journey, in the beginning...

This accounts for humans being fascinated with all of creation. The types and how they interact with each other. The curiosity of discovering other "new" thoughts that were created before them...

Note: The Unconditional Love part of the Spirit creates all its thoughts, male and female versions of the same thought species. This gives all individual created thought species; the experience of sharing in the Creative Making Journey together, with the Unconditional Love part of the Spirit. The male and female same species companions, have the desire to pro-create and raise their children together.

Note: The Self-Centered Love part of the Spirit creates only one version of the species, and or hijacks a fetus. Each of its species tend to believe that they are both male and female, at the same time. They feel like a more "superior" species. But in reality, they are Self-Centered to their cores. And have no desire to be apart of the creative making journey. They have NO desire to procreate together, let alone have the patience to raise their children.

The first male and female humans along with the other humans with core numbers of 10 vibrating to go lower; were just realizing that this is what the Unconditional Love part of the Spirit was referring to. In losing their senses; this would help them in learning the meaning of these five words, the Unconditional Love part of the Spirit uses in the conversations with them. These words being: Faith, Perseverance, Compassion, Forgiveness and Peace…

Aaaah…

We are going to have, physical sight to learn faith, to go through the whole Creative Making Journey together and throughout all eternity. This will give Insight to those who are blind to faith.

If I'm blind to faith then having Insight will help me see like a child.

We are going to have; physical hearing to learn perseverance, to go through the whole Creative Making Journey together and throughout all eternity. This will give Accountability to those who are deaf to perseverance.

If I'm deaf to perseverance then having Accountability will help me hear like an adult.

We are going to have; physical taste to learn compassion, to go through the whole Creative Making Journey together and throughout all eternity. This will give Unconditional Love to those who are flavorless to compassion.

If I'm flavorless to compassion then having Unconditional Love will help me taste like a friend.

We are going to have; physical touch to learn forgiveness, to go through the whole Creative Making Journey together and throughout all eternity. This will help us to be an Extrovert to those who are numb to forgiveness.

If I'm numb to forgiveness then being an Extrovert will help me touch like a companion.

We are going to have; physical smell to learn peace, to go through the whole Creative Making Journey together and throughout all eternity. This will help us to be Good Teachers to those who are Fragrantless to peace.

If I'm fragrantless to peace then being a Good Teacher will help me smell like parent.

Another way of Applying these are:

When the Self-Centered Love part of the Spirit makes us blind to faith, being a Child with the Unconditional Love part of the Spirit will help us to **SEE** FAITH and **HAVE** INSIGHT.

When the Self-Centered Love part of the Spirit makes us deaf to perseverance, being an Adult with the Unconditional Love part of the Spirit will help us to **HEAR** PERSEVERANCE and **HAVE** ACCOUNTABILITY.

When the Self-Centered Love part of the Spirit makes us tasteless to compassion, being a Friend with the Unconditional Love part of the Spirit will help us to **TASTE** COMPASSION and **HAVE** UNCONDITIONAL LOVE.

When the Self-Centered Love part of the Spirit makes us numb to forgiveness, being a Companion with the Unconditional Love part of the Spirit will help us to **TOUCH** FORGIVENESS and **BE AN** EXTROVERT.

When the Self-Centered Love part of the Spirit makes us fragrantless to peace, being a Parent with the Unconditional Love part of the Spirit will help us to **SMELL** PEACE and **BE A** Good Teacher.

Deep but profound...

COMPONENTS of the THESE FIVE WORDS:

Faith: Child, *Sight*, Insight.
Perseverance: Adult, *Hearing*, Accountability.
Compassion: Friend, *Taste*, Unconditional Love.
Forgiveness: Companion, *Touch*, Extrovert.
Peace: Parent, *Smell*, Teacher.

Self-Centered Love part of the Spirit CREATES:

Blindness vs Sight - Faith - Insight.
Deafness vs Hearing - Perseverance - Accountability.
Flavorless vs Taste - Compassion – Unconditional Love.
Numbness vs Touch - Forgiveness - Extrovert.
Fragrantless vs Smell - Peace - Teacher.

NOTE: The Self-Centered Love part of the Spirit creatures and or hijacked fetuses; have **zero desire** to understand faith, perseverance, compassion, forgiveness and peace.

Wow... The first male and female humans, along with others stopped. Slowly and gently becoming at peace, with a surreal feeling to it. They had never have experienced this feeling before. *Period.* And now understood more than ever, why they had to become physically created thoughts...

They gently and compassionately looked at their companions and their friends, with eyes of complete understanding. And more than ever knowing with all their cores; that this Creative

Making Journey was necessary to complete their relationships, with the Unconditional Love part of the Spirit and with each other.

Relishing all the previous baby steps they took together and now especially this one...

*They all **busted out** with **humming** their favorite musical sounds...*

This went on for a while.

This moved the Unconditional Love part of the Spirit, to the point Its Core *started crying*. Those that were humming, saw the tears of the Unconditional Love part of the Spirit and begin crying themselves. It was a surreal; it's ok now, **we get it** crying...

This sensation for ALL of Creation with the Unconditional Love part of the Spirit was completely new; and deepened the density of the Unconditional Love, in the cores of all of them.

These ... I'm on a roll, dude. This is going to be too freaking easy.... *Aaaah...* Feeling that eternity peace and quiet already... *Aaaah... Aaaaaaaaaaaah!... self-induced trance* moment, that the Self-Centered Love part of the Spirit was having...

Was shattered by those same humming musical sounds; by all of creation...now being physical creation, that the Unconditional Love part of the Spirit had to create.

MMMMMM... said; The Self-Centered Love part of the Spirit as it snapped out of its trance, in a loud thunderous deep tone.

It was so loud, that the thunderous deep tone penetrated into all of creation's core. Creation stopped humming, and their tears of joy turned to tears of sadness.

Now this wasn't their first time... most of creation ignored it. It was easier to ignore it, this second time. When ignoring the Self-Centered Love part of the Spirit, this strengthens the density of their cores even more. Pure Physical Unconditional Love naturally repels Self-Centered Love part of the Spirit...

For the first male and female humans and the others, it wasn't so easy. This time; that sound created a more-deeper form of Doubt, fusing with their humming sounds... however they were able to shake it loose from their cores. Some fragments of the **MMMM** tones were embedding in their cores. These fragments were Conditioning them, to accept Mental Abuse is OK.

Now this cycle of the first male and female humans and the others; letting go the sounds coming from the Self-Centered Love part of the Spirit, continued. Some let it loose more easily than others...

Those who tried to focus on letting it go, was conditioning their cores with deeper densities of Unconditional Love. The fragments were just building up at a slower rate, then the others...

What encouraged them to continue to try releasing the sounds; was the looking at the other creation, that was ignoring the sounds. They weren't being affected by it at all. Period...

The rest of the humans, was beginning to accept this mental abuse as the "new" norm. Some dealt with it, others started to take it out on other humans.

"Aaaaaah... I'm back and so is the Adrenaline Rushes; I get from doing this, are kicking in. Oh Yah Baby! .... Yeeehaaa!" said the Self-Centered Love part of the Spirit...

*"***Hmmm** those physical babies. I've got to stop the babies from

being born. *Hmmm...*

"My sounds that enter their cores are affecting them. I will create super tiny creatures; within my sounds, and they will cause death to their bodies and babies. *Perfect...*

"I AM **SOOOO** PROUD OF MYSELF! The Self-Centered Love part of the Spirit was relishing in itself...

"Hmmm. **I CAN OUT CREATE** the Unconditional Love part of the Spirit with less effort and frustration. To the point; it will give up and come back to me and say, I'm sorry for messing up our PURE SILENCE AND PEACE...

"Love it. I'm a genius!...

"**Oooooo better yet.** *I might as well destroy* the Unconditional Love part of the Spirit for once and all. When it starts to regret even wanting to have eternal physical friends, it will be at its weakest moment. I will destroy Unconditional Love part of the Spirit. Then I will NEVER have to worry about the Unconditional Love part of the Spirit, getting second thoughts and try creating physical friends again.

"**PERFECT!**"

The Self-Centered Love part of the Spirit had more confidence in itself, than it ever had. It's Arrogancy was an ALL TIME high. It was totally at peace in destroying 110+% of the Unconditional Love part of the Spirit. To the point, this would be its Guarantee of being Eternally by itself. Forever. **Period.**

Note: All these words that are in bold that are spoken by the Self-Centered Love part of the Spirit; were penetrating the cores of the physical creation, that weren't ignoring them.

That last word **PERFECT** that the Self-Centered Love part of the Spirit, said with all of it's Core. Went straight to the Core of the Unconditional Love part of the Spirit. **INSTANTLY.** The Unconditional Love part of the Spirit, NEVER felt that from the Self-Centered Love part of the Spirit…

All those EONS and EONS that they were together; without zero thoughts of creating friends, the Self-Centered Love part of the Spirit never ever thought that…

This sadden the Unconditional Love part of the Spirit to it's Core. So much so, all of creation could feel it. This was too much for them to bear and all the humans; even the first male and female humans, core numbers all dropped down to 9. Many others dropped down to 6 and 5…

Those who dropped down to 6 and 5, lost sight of seeing all of creation. They could no longer see their other spirit friends, yet to be physically created. All of their senses were way different now. They never felt this EVER in their total existence, from being a thought to now a physical creation…

Some couldn't handle the change to the point; they were agreeing to let others take their physical lives, so that their spirits could return to their spirit friends…

This tore up the Unconditional Love part of the Spirit **BIG TIME!** This was the first time it ever doubted itself… Then seeing some of these physical-creation taking their lives, to set their spirits free… was even more disheartlng…

The Unconditional Love part of the Spirit knew it was going to have to endure some pain itself, but didn't realize it was going to be this bad. It's the worse pain that it ever felt…

The Self-Centered Love part of the Spirit was looking at the Unconditional Love part of the Spirit's Core. And said, "I'm cleaning up all these created-thoughts and destroying everything you thought of. Then I'm destroying you for once and for all." ... **PERIOD!**

This shredded every last hope and desire, that the Unconditional Love part of the Spirit had in its Core...

All of creation felt and heard, what was being said to the Unconditional Love part of the Spirit. Even those who cores dropped down to 6s and 5s.

Everyone was silent, even the Self-Centered Love part of the Spirit and Unconditional Love part of the Spirit.

It was the most deafen sound/thought there has ever been...

The first male and female humans looked at each other; witnessing both sides of physical creation, with their cores at a 9 in the crux. Their male Pitbull friend came up to them, sensing their anguish in their cores. The male Pitbull laid its head on their laps. They gently pushed the male Pitbull away. This crux moment was commanding all of their attention. This was the first and most detrimental problem; that the first male and female humans ever had to deal with...

The female Pitbull companion of the male Pitbull; looked at its Companion male Pitbull in the eyes, with the look **yup**. *Perfect time to do this...*

The density of Unconditional Love in their cores, is one of the highest in all of creation. It's right up there next to the Unconditional Love part of the Spirit's.

Instantly the male and female Pitbulls had flipped the first male and female humans on their backs. And laid on them with all their weight... so that *they couldn't* get up.

The first male and female humans, were surprised and shocked at the same time. They had never had that experience before, with their Pitbull friends... Their facial expressions were priceless...

Everyone that was around them; including those yet to be physically made, busted out laughing. It was the ***most adorable sight*** they had ever seen, up to this point...

While the male and female Pitbull companions, had this look of *satisfaction* on their faces...

Plus; all four of them, got this deeper interacting enriching physical experience. To the point; everyone around them were speechless, at awe and was wanting to experience this same connection they were...

The first male and female humans looked at each other, and giggled. *Relaxed*. And begin to think about this crux moment, like any other previous baby step...

They were understanding each other thoughts and agreeing. This must be the Adult Stage we're moving into; in learning the meaning of the words the Unconditional Love part of the Spirit speaks to us, but don't know what they mean. ***Aaaaah....***

Their male and female Pitbull companion friends was not moving anytime soon and ***LOVING IT***...

The first male and female humans said it out loud, at the same time... **PERSEVERANCE!** We need to be Accountable to ourselves, to see this Creative Making Journey through to the end. **PERIOD...**

With that; they both gently tapped their male and female companion Pitbull friends on their butts, and said ***"Ok, Get Up!"*** ...

The male and female companion Pitbulls looked at each other. Yup. They are in the right Mindset now. They got up and started wagging their tails BIG TIME! Then those All around them; even those that were not physical created yet, ***BUSTED out***

Dancing. They were all happy and celebrating this moment of understanding, what the word Perseverance means...

This is the first time, they All experience celebrating this breakthrough in their physical bodies. It was so sincere, that it started to heal their cores. Those on 9 went back to 10. Those who were on 6s and 5s, went back up to 8s and 9s. They were all amazed on how easy it was to self-heal their cores...

When Unconditional Love is shared, it is truly stronger than Self-Centered Love. Just by persevering through the affects, of Self-Centered Love on their physical lives...

They all stopped dancing. The first male human knelt down and kissed his male Pitbull friend. Watching; the first female human knelt down as well, and kissed the female Pitbull. And Thanked Them for being sensitive to their pain, stress and perplexities.

All of creation started *humming* all those musical sounds, that they love to hear from the beginning of their journey. No matter how many times.

Back when the first male and female humans said **PERSEVERANCE** out Loud together, that grabbed the total attention of both the Self-Centered Love part of the Spirit and the Unconditional Love part of the Spirit... They were into totally absorbing every moment of this experience, with creation.

The Unconditional Love part of the Spirit's tore up Core started to self-heal, while its doubt slowly dissipated. This infinite amount of doubt almost crushed the Unconditional Love part of the Spirit. As the doubt was dissipating; the Unconditional Love part of the Spirit, started to feel more stronger than ever. It smiled. Realizing when Unconditional Love is exercised, it becomes much more-stronger. ***Hmmm...***

The Self-Centered Love part of the Spirit was shocked; at how fast the physical creation could heal their cores back, when they ignore their problem. And focus on having good Unconditional Love interacting times together. *Hmmm...*

"I will have to modify my strategy, to making sure I'm always dividing them into groups. I'll create and get them to justify; having a group over them, is in their "best" interest. Meanwhile in the background it will keep them divided. This will increase my odds in succeeding…

"This is going to take a little longer than I previously thought." Said the Self-Centered Love part of the Spirit.

As the surreal, with more confidence than ever humming continued…

The Unconditional Love part of the Spirit and Self-Centered Love part of the Spirit, looked intently into each other's Cores. **Both Realizing for the first time**; they both now have a force to reckon with…

For the Unconditional Love part of the Spirit, it buckled down and *embraced perseverance* with all of its Core; to seeing this Creative Making Journey to the end with All of Creation… It was before, but in the thought mode. Whereas now this is now in the physical doing mode.

Example: Wanting to ride a horse with no experience is different than actually physically riding a horse with experience. **Two different animals.** Pardon the pun. That was punny. *Footnote: Speaking from personal experience.*

By the Unconditional Love part of the Spirit embracing this for the long haul; with all of its Core, its Cores Density grew infinitely more.

For the Self-Centered Love part of the Spirit; *it was temporarily second guessing itself, while the Unconditional Love part of the Spirit's Core grew infinitely stronger with more Unconditional Love...*

For a moment; the Self-Centered Love part of the Spirit was wishing the physical creation, never let it out of its abyss...

Snapped out of it. "**NOPE.** It's them or me. They ARE All gone or I AM. Not dealing with this drama for the rest of eternity. **NO WAY...**

hmmm...

"When I created doubt it worked, but it wasn't strong enough. I need to *commit to persevering* through; the physical creation's reactions, in taking this to the very end...

"Never second guessing myself again" ... As the Self-Centered Love part of the Spirit was saying that, its Core grew with infinitely more Self-Centered Love.

AAAAAAH.... Perfect timing. It laughed.

"OK. Back to Destroying All of Creation and Along with their side kick, the Unconditional Love part of the Spirit... it laughed again. "Piece of Cake!"

"*Ooooo*. I'll make them a "Way to Go!" cake and when they all go to eat it, it will blow up in their faces." As the Self-Centered Love part of the Spirit was saying that. It felt reassured in living to see the day; where it would be at total peace again, living in all of eternity by itself.

There was a deep sobering silence throughout all of creation and with both the Unconditional Love and Self-Centered Love parts of the Spirit. Knowing it was the Self-Centered Love part of the Spirit's move - next.

This time; All of their resolves harden and embedded in their cores, in going to the finish line.

The Self-Centered part of the Spirit, didn't waste anymore time in *la la land*. It went to work creating new Self-Centered Love creatures and it was getting addictive.

It started out in the "outer" perimeters of creation for a soft intro. Focusing on amping up its adrenaline rushes, in the process…

Dang. It's not that easy. I can create these Self-Centered Love species, but they're not moving. *They are just lying there…* Why is Unconditional Love part of the Spirit's creation moving around on their own?

Deeper looking into it; the Self-Centered Love part of the Spirit realized they had their unique own spirits, that kept the body alive and moving around…

Double Dang… this complicates my problem, and makes a bigger mess to clean up in the end…

Hmmm… Got it. I will live in all the Self-Centered Love creation, I make. That way I can be in total charge of ALL the situations and backup contingent plans, in this controlled demolition. This "energy" that keeps my Self-Centered Love creation alive, **will be the soul** of the creature. When my creatures are no more of use, my soul can leave their bodies…

Plus … I can create beings/creatures that will appear to them as ascended beings, who will guide them in the opposite direction of their life journeys.

This soul – me – will make it easier for me, to connect all my creation together. Regardless of where they are and what they are doing, in all of creation. **Perfect… PLUS** keep my narratives going without missing a beat, no matter how many times I get disconnected from it. There's no needing to get "new" recruits.

Even when it's time to "kill" the creature, all I have to do is leave its body. And start all over in another creature, that is created from where I left off.

Oops... Another problem. How am I going to "pro-create" more of the same species, when I don't have male and female versions of the same species?... *dang.*

I will create male and female versions of the same species, to put them/us on autopilot. With the smaller species (insects, bacteria, etc.), I'll be able to create swarms of them...

This is making this harder than what it needs to be...

The larger ones; I'll create them on the planets I create, so I can do this away from the Unconditional Love part of the Spirit's creation. *Perfect.*

Now the last problem. How can I infiltrate, the rest of the Unconditional Love part of the Spirit's creation?

The Self-Centered Love part of the Spirit smiles... I will hijack their own baby making process, they have. Watching for the right time; when the spirit created thoughts are about jump, into their physical bodies. I will push them aside and take their place. The parents of each species; that the Unconditional Love part of the Spirit creates, won't see it coming. Especially when their cores are below number 9...

I will first condition them with mental and physical abuse, so that it will be easier to hijack their babies.

Perfect. All the important areas are covered.

Moving forward. I will keep hammering them with doubt; to condition them to accepting this mental abuse, is the new normal from now on... Until their core numbers get below 6, so that they can't sense me doing it anymore.

Meanwhile I will build up the smaller "insect and bacteria" species, to "plague" them with...

While their being distracted, I will build up my species throughout all of creation. In areas where I can create my own planet echo systems, that feed on destroying their environments. This will allow them/us to build up strength, to wage destruction on the Unconditional Love part of the Spirit's species.

AAAAH.... This is going to be cheap entertainment, while I'm destroying everything that the Unconditional Love part of the Spirit Created.... *Beautiful.*

It wasn't long the touching sensations; that the Self-Centered part of the Spirit was getting while destroying creation, was kicking in. GETTING THESE SENSATIONS; BECAME THE MAIN motive to destroying creation, all the more...

The more the mass destruction it did; the higher the touch sensations, it felt throughout its whole infinite CORE being. This too, was never felt before creation was physically created...

When the Self-Centered Love part of the Spirt wasn't mass destroying creation; it would begin to have anxiety, that would lead to depression...

After the Self-Centered Love part of Spirit was released in all of physical creation, the Unconditional Love part of the Spirit's...

Faith, Perseverance, Compassion, Forgiveness and Peace *multiplied even stronger* than what it was; when the Unconditional Love part of the Spirit contained the Self-Centered Love part of the Spirit, so that it could have room for its created thoughts into physical existence...

As the Unconditional Love part of the Spirit's Core got stronger, the Self-Centered Love part of the Spirit would experience anxiety and depression.

NOTE: The cycle is the same every time. It can be calculated and determined; by what part of the cycle the Self-Centered Love part of the Spirit is in, by those whose senses are being weakened and restored.

Once the Self-Centered Love part of the Spirit felt confident; in all of creatures, planets, celestial systems and technology it created, it took a break. Looking over everything it created felt rewarding. These accomplishments, strengthen the Core of the Self-Centered Love part of the Spirit.

Note: In time passing; the Self-Centered Love part of the Spirit would realize that this strength would be a fake strength, and add to its depression.

At first all of creation of the Unconditional Love part of the Spirit; was devastated by the destruction, of what the Self-Centered Love part of the Spirit was doing to them. Those created thoughts that were not physically created yet, felt helpless. Witnessing the destruction of their friends...

Over time; the rest of the creation minus the humans, **would work together in routing out** the Self-Centered Love creatures and those that got their babies hijacked...

Every new generation, the Self-Centered Love part of the Spirit would try again. The humans with core numbers below 9 would just assume, that certain species were "bad" and be on their guard against. In reality the species had one "bad" apple amongst them.

Examples: Alligators, Lions, Wolves, Sharks, Octopuses, etc. When these creatures are showed Unconditional Love, they cautiously compassionately reciprocate Unconditional Love back. Being abused by the Self-Centered Love throughout the generations; they have automatically taken the position of not trusting, until proven otherwise.

The smaller creatures that the Unconditional Love part of the Spirit created; after a few generations in the beginning, automatically went on the offensive.

Examples: The good insects would always be looking out for each other. The good bacteria would automatically dispose the bad bacteria. At times the Self-Centered Love part of the Spirit; through its human bodies would convince the other humans, that the bad bacteria are the good bacteria and the good bacteria is the bad bacteria…

When that wasn't enough the Self-Centered Love part of the Spirit through its human bodies; would convince the other humans, to use certain liquids/powders to kill the "bad" bacteria. In reality those liquids/powders would kill and or detain, the good bacteria from disposing the bad bacteria automatically.

Over a few generations the Self-Centered Love part of the Spirit; *gave up* on trying to destroy all of creation, and directly focused 98% of its time on the humans…

After the first global annihilation of creation, it realized this even more. The Self-Centered Love part of the Spirit had time for a break, to relish its accomplishment…

Aaaah… a taste of the peace to come. Woooohoooo!

The Unconditional Love part of the Spirit was soberly grieving but proud of its creation; in persevering all the more, in their conflicts with the Self-Centered Love part of the Spirit…

From time to time; the Unconditional Love part of the Spirit would look directly at the Core of the Self-Centered Love part of the Spirit, with a surreal peaceful confidence of you're wasting your time. Why don't you stop now, call it good *bro* and give up...

After seeing that look from the Unconditional Love part of the Spirit; the Self-Centered Love part of the Spirit would try even harder, to destroy all of creation...

Thinking harder on upgrading its strategy. I'll focus on those creation with the lowest core numbers. Hmmm... it's the humans. Why?

Silence... More Silence... The Self-Centered Love part of the Spirit annulated creation so bad, that it had a lot of time to think...

The Self-Centered Love part of the Spirit went back over this whole journey; from the beginning when the Unconditional Love part of the Spirit, wanted to create eternal friends. *Hmmm.*

Aaaah... It's the first male and female human of the humans. They were the ones who opened the door of my abyss. And They insisted on looking for that human of the future; that would release me from the creation, to go back into my abyss. **DANG!**...

I was so busy destroying creation; and making my own creation to help me destroy creation, I forgot ALL about that... **DOUBLE DANG!!**

I need to go back and focus on just those human babies.

I'll create "believable" religions to be normalize amongst the humans, and that its normal to worship "ascended" beings. These will be surface distractions, for my soul humans to "sacrifice" babies to my "ascended" beings. *Plus.* I'll have my soul humans; set up different types of human trafficking networks, to feed the sacrificing... *Perfect.*

Now it makes more sense; why I'm having a harder time destroying the rest of creation, because their cores are 10 to

9 and never waver any lower. Whereas during the last few moments of this global annihilation, the humans' cores were on 1s and 2s...

Loving it... This will be a good time to introduce; my ascended soul beings from other celestial areas, while the population of the humans are at near extinction levels...

Wooooohooooo! It's time to have some enjoyable entertainment, while destroying ALL of creation... Pat myself on my Core Dude!...

I've been taking myself way too seriously. Getting all stressed up for what? I can distract the humans with cheap entertainment. While destroying them in the process...

And just maybe...just maybe irritate the Unconditional Love part of the Spirit, at the same time. **Oh dude, It's Flip the Script Time... I'M ALL IN.**

ALRIGHT! Let's get started...

Some of the humans that survived the global annihilation; were intrigued by the "ascended" beings, being in their presence. It took their minds off of all the loses they just incurred; with their loved ones and their current condition of Earth. This gave them "hope" in rebuilding, their lives and communities... but they didn't realize it was a soft intro to religion, centralized authorities and free roaming human enslavement.

The Self-Centered Love part of the Spirit would use abstract descriptive words like: holy, almighty, worthy, etc. It hijacked All of Creation's humming; with the Unconditional Love part of the Spirit and got them to sing "spiritual" hymns, without the humming...

Plus hijacked All of Creation raising their hands and gently moving their fingers tips; to rub the Unconditional Love part of the Spirit, as one way of saying thankyou for creating us... The Self-Centered Love part of the Spirit informed them; that these "Ascended" Beings are "holy" and they need to raise their hands, to acknowledging they are.

The Self-Centered Love part of the Spirit was laughing behind their backs. Thinking this is way too easy, and a whole lot funnier in the process...

The rest of the humans that survived were introduce to the rest of the celestial creation; that the Unconditional Love part of the Spirit created beyond "Earth." ...

This gave the Unconditional Love part of the Spirit the opportunity to reintroduced itself; to the humans that survived with most of their cores being 1s, 2s, 3s with some on 6s to 8s. Even those that were not physically created, was with them. Some of those humans that had their cores on 8s, saw glimpses of those yet to be physically created...

This was a self-healing moment for rest of the humans, those yet to be physically created and the Unconditional Love part of the Spirit.

Before they all got deep into this new moment of their Creative Making Journey together; they quieted themselves and *started humming* their music sounds that they still love to hear, as they first did in the beginning...

The Unconditional Love part of the Spirit was so much more than ever proud of them; for being at peace, in moving forward in baby steps. Getting use to the cycles of Perseverance and seeing where they are at, in this learning what these words mean.

A few generations down from the line of the first male and

female humans, spoke up and said, "By the looks of it, we've got Perseverance mastered. We should now look at mastering Compassion, since we're at this devastating moment in our journey. And if we remember right Mastering Compassion, allows us to be better Friends to each other" ...

They all began to smile, especially the first male and female humans. This was their great great grand children saying this. The first male and female humans, looked deep into each other's eyes. And was hearing each other thinking. This is priceless, seeing our children's future generations, understanding the meaning of these words...

Just think, if we would have never decided to open the door of the abyss; we would have never enjoyed this, as much as we Do RIGHT Now...

They leaned over to each other and hugged, while everyone was watching them. Some could hear their thoughts and others saw it on their faces...

Thus; they were starting the understanding the word Compassion part of the journey, with a hug.

The **Unconditional Love** part of the Spirit, **spoke up** and said, "Sweet... It's time to show you some inside resources; that will give you the advantage point, if you and or future generations find their backs up against a wall."

They were all smiling ear to ear. Even though they didn't have a clue; what the Unconditional Love part of the Spirit was talking about, they knew *it was going to be fantastic.* It's like they've experienced these-baby step patterns so much; that if they could read what the Unconditional Love part of the Spirit was going to say next, they would...

The Unconditional Love part of the Spirit's Core was smiling...

Knowing what they were thinking.

They were all in Silence, enjoying this moment with their favorite humming music sounds…

The Unconditional Love part of the Spirit started to cry, with finite tears of joy. And defiantly having no regrets, in its first thoughts of creating eternal friends. The infinite tears of joy were so great; that they fell from the atmosphere, like rain. When the "rain" tears of joy fell on their lips, they tasted sweet. When the "rain" tears of joy fell on the devasted and parched land; the trees and other vegetation, started to grow extremely lush in a matter of minutes…

They were all amazed of what just happened, in front of their physical bodies. *Continued humming* their favorite musical sounds…

The other humans that were entranced, with the Self-Centered Love part of the Spirit's "Ascended" creatures. When the infinite tears of joy landed on their lips, it broke them out of their trances…

For a moment; they saw everything as it was. Some of them were angry at themselves, for falling for these lies. They picked up what they had and left with their families, to go find the other humans…

The rest of them; thought maybe they were seeing the future, and turned their eyes back on the "Ascended" creatures…

The Self-Centered Love part of the Spirit in and out of its "Ascended" creatures, knew instantly what was happening. But was taken off guard on how to react…

This was the first time that the Unconditional Love part of the Spirit; subtly *made a soft intro,* into the core of the Self-Centered

Love part of the Spirit's strategy in destroying creation…

The Self-Centered Love part of the Spirit's in having its fun strategy, just got cracked in half. It was angry and infuriated… and just realized, it was under estimating the Unconditional Love part of the Spirit. It assumed Unconditional Love part of the Spirit, had a push over mindset…

This snapped the Self-Centered Love part of the Spirit out of its own trance. When it was looking at its "Ascended" creatures, they were all slummed over and laying on the ground…

The humans around them had been trying to wake them up, but no avail…

Now the Self-Centered Love part of the Spirit; felt stupid and embarrassed, but these humans couldn't see him… "That's way cool they can't see me." It thought…

Waiting for the most realistic moment to "reawaken" the "Ascended" creatures from their "sleep." …

The humans that stayed around; started humming the music sounds they like to hum, with their other humans…

"**Perfect!**" "Sweet holy slice bananas!" The Self-Centered Love part of the Spirit thought. "I'll hijacked their humming as a way to awaken my "Ascended" creatures!" "**Perfect. Wooooohoooo! Back in Business Bro!**" …

The Self-Centered Love part of the Spirit, "awoken" the "Ascended" creature's bodies…

The humans that was close by; humming for some time now, immediately stopped. They were amazed and sincerely thought, their humming awoken the "Ascended" creatures…

The Self-Centered Love part of the Spirit as the "soul" in the

"Ascended" creature's bodies, began to echo their humming sounds back to them. One of them stopped and said "Thank You! We had fallen into a deep sleep; and enjoying it, as you witnessed it yourselves. Whenever you see us like this; please start humming those beautiful sounds, to awaken us…

"We are your friends and we want you to feel relaxed around us." the Self-Centered Love part of the Spirit, said through them…

Phew. That was close. I have to solidify my *stand by* contingent plans; to always be expecting the Unconditional Love part of the Spirit sneaking into any part of my strategies, while destroying all of creation…

The Unconditional Love part of the Spirit stopped crying, physical tears of joy. It had never done that ever, up until now. It was getting tingling sensations that it never had. This too was confirmation to the Unconditional Love part of the Spirit; had made the right choice in continuing this Creating Making Journey, with All of Creation…

All of the creation and the humans that were around; along with those yet to be physically created, never felt the goodness of Unconditional Love part of the Spirit at this density ever. It had such a huge impact on the human cores at 1s 2s 3s; it strengthen them up to 4s 5s and 6s…

When the Unconditional Love part of the Spirit saw and felt this, it smiled. Then said, "*Nope.* I'm not going to cry more physical tears of joy, like that for a while." …

The humans that were around, were like that's cool.

Then the Unconditional Love part of the Spirit started to sniffle; like it was going to start to cry, like that again…

The humans that were around, their eyes got like real big! Like dude? You just said you weren't! …

The Unconditional Love part of the Spirit **BUSTED OUT** LAUGHING. "Gotcha you!" …

The humans; All the Creation and those yet to be physically created, ALL **BUSTED OUT** LAUGHING *too*.

They all reached another precious moment; in their Creating Making Journey together, and this time they were able to celebrate it with humor…

This too was a whole new experience; they all had never felt before. It was priceless. They All could feel in their cores; that they knew the journey might get rougher at times, but their going to make it to the end. And now a whole lot easier with humor…

Instead of busting out humming this time, like in the past… they all continue laughing together.

The Self-Centered Love part of the Spirit heard them, when they all BUST OUT LAUGHING HARD. It went straight to its Core. This time it was planning for this, so it ignored it. And its "Ascended" creatures didn't collapse…

Out of the blue; the "Ascended" creatures busted out laughing with no reason. The humans around them, were like what's so funny?

The Unconditional Love part of the Spirit stopped laughing; with all of creation and said, "You Ready to go see those Resources Now?" …

The humans around them nodded their heads yes. The humans; all of creation and those yet to be physically created, followed the Unconditional Love part of the Spirit to the door of the Abyss.

As they were All getting closer; the humans and all of creation were getting more apprehensive…

The Unconditional Love part of the Spirit; could even feel it radiate from their cores.

As their faces flushed out; the Unconditional Love part of the Spirit spoke up, "This will let you know, how high your cores are. The higher your cores are in Unconditional Love; it won't even affect you."

All of creation and some of the humans, didn't flush out much. The rest of the humans did; and especially those humans who left the group, that was entranced with the Self-Centered Love part of the Spirit "Ascended" creatures.

At first some of them got flash backs, to the very first time the Abyss door was opened up. Now those parents/ great grand parents are with their children and grandchildren. The generations were extremely fascinated, to see what their parents and grandparents did. But were being cautious, seeing the looks on their faces…

"That's just a side note. The real reason why we're here is; I want to show you a tool that will give you an advantage, over the Self-Centered part of the Spirit."

At that; most of the humans and all of creation went off to the side to play and tell stories of what it was like, on the day they opened the door to the Abyss.

The first male and female humans, with a few of their grandchildren and all those yet to be physically created stayed.

The Unconditional Love part of the Spirit continued, "Most of the time; all you have to do is look in the window, of the door to the Abyss. Remember what it was like before?" ….

The first male and female humans nodded their heads; with memories of the Self-Centered Love part of the Spirit, screaming out the door like no other. The quickly shook their heads; to shake those thoughts out, of the conversation they were having now...

"Now. Go ahead and look in the window now, to see the difference." ...

The first male human took the hand of the first female human, and went over to the window of the door to the Abyss. Their children and grandchildren were watching them...

The first male and female humans; looked into each other's eyes and gently squeezed each other's hands. Then turned their heads and looked intently into the window, to see what was going on. This time they were well experienced; and the first-time shock values, were all worn away...

They stopped at looked at each other. They were listening to each other thoughts. This is exactly what's going on NOW. Anywhere on this Earth, everywhere in all of creation and through out all of the universal expanse of creation. They were seeing in real time; what the Self-Centered Love part of the Spirit was doing, in and with the creatures it created...

The Unconditional Love part of the Spirit knew what they were thinking and said, "Exactly!" "Now you don't have to wonder what the Self-Centered Love part of the Spirit is doing; and where it's focusing on, to destroy all of creation... It's so busy now; that it doesn't have time and or be scared, that we are looking at it right now." ...

"Now as a footnote we need to remember this; when we reach tipping point in All of creation, getting excited about knowing how to move their cores numbers from the 1s, 2s, etc. to 9s and 10s in Unconditional Love. The Self-Centered Love part of the Spirit is *going to get **more angier***, than it has ever been before...

"But at that point it won't matter to all of creation; because the strengthening of their cores in Unconditional Love will supersede, what the Self-Centered Love part of the Spirit can do to you...

"Always remember the Strength of Unconditional Love is always stronger than Self-Centered Love. **PERIOD.** Remember when I condensed, ALL of the Self-Centered Love part of the Spirit into this Abyss? It was angry at me when I was doing it, BUT I ignored it....

"**Example:** Think of a scary moment you two experienced together?... Now think about how you two got through it together...Now how do you both feel about that experience?" ...

The human's spoke right up, "We feel a whole lot stronger and are having a more enriching relationship from it!"

The Unconditional Love part of the Spirit smiled, "That is a perfect example of Unconditional Love is Stronger than Self-Centered Love... The only thing the Self-Centered Love part of the Spirit has is Fear; in hoping All of Creation will be too scared, to hold on to Unconditional Love... **The two advantages** the Self-Centered Love part of the Spirit has; *first*, is when your cores are below 5. Creation loses and or starts to lose its premonition skills. Looking into the window of the door to the Abyss will help somewhat, but for the most part... not. *Second*, it's creatures that it is creating. They can inflict a lot of mental and physical damage on you, if you don't see them coming for you...

"If you noticed when you just were looking in the window; the Self-Centered Love part of the Spirit, was doing soft intros to those other humans. These soft intros are conditioning the humans, to believe in the lies of the Self-Centered Love part of the Spirit. Its goal is to lead them to slow deaths, and or slaughters. As you saw in the window the first time, just before you released it from its Abyss...

"When my infinite tears of joy were raining down on the earth. Some of those humans who had higher core numbers, tasted the sweet rain and got instant glimpses of the truth. Packed up their families and belongings and returned to us...

"During the Full-on slot Slaughters; you and your loved ones might have to take a lot of sacrifices, in protecting your kind." ...

Silence...

The first male and female humans was absorbing all these revelations in, as vital tools for this Creative Making Journey together. They were at total peace; in remembering all those baby steps moments, they have been sharing together from the beginning.

They smiled at the Unconditional Love part of the Spirit and said, "Thank You!" ...

Turning to their children and grandchildren; to gently introduce them to looking in the window, of the door to the Abyss...

This moment with their children and grandchildren; was not only healing to the first male and female humans, but also deepen their enriching relationships with their generations. It's like all the hardships they went through; were well worth persevering through them, to be able to enjoy this moment.

The Unconditional Love part of the Spirit was enjoying this moment as well. Seeing this; confirmed its decision once again, creating eternal friends was the Best Decision it Ever Made. Seeing these generations enjoying and interacting with one another, was like the Unconditional Love part of the Spirit interacting individually with them.

No one was rushing this baby step moment together...

The first male and female humans was having such a great time together as a family, the rest of all of the creation joined in. This bonding moment they had with each other, moved their cores up 1 to 2 numbers…

Even the other humans that came back to be with them; was enjoying the healing of their cores together so much, that now they were feeling sorry for those who stayed behind…

Towards the end of this moment they were sharing together; the first male and female humans turned and asked the Unconditional Love part of the Spirit, "Is there anything else you want to show us?"

The Unconditional Love part of the Spirit *smiled,* "Most defiantly… When your cores are in 9s and 10s, you can open the door and go into the Abyss. You can go to and anywhere in; the Self-Centered Love part of the Spirit has created, instantly. This will infinitely speed up your saving those who need to be saved; but can't help themselves enough, to do it on their own…

"Would you like to test it out?" …

The first male and female humans looked at each other with eyes of excitement, especially knowing their families are in a good place now. All of creation was supportive. Along with those yet to be physically created. Then turned back to the Unconditional Love part of the Spirit and said, "**YES**." And with no Doubt.

This moment with their families, temporarily put all of their cores on 9s and 10s. Even those humans that returned.

The first male and female humans could feel the hurt from the humans that returned; that they had loved ones, that didn't come with them.

The Unconditional Love part of the Spirit said to the first male and female humans, "I'll Go with You." …

"You remember that the door can only be opened by a male and female companion, who are in agreement and in one mind? And that both their hands must be together, on the door handle?"

"**YES**" and before you knew it; the first male and female humans opened the door, and went into the Abyss along with the Unconditional Love part of the Spirit.

As long as they ignored the Self-Centered Love part of the Spirit's consciousness; the first male and female humans did ok, navigating to where the other humans were. They were thinking; where are the lost humans and bam, they were right there instantly. Just as the Unconditional Love part of the Spirit said…

They all smiled at each other. And began to watch how the Self-Centered Love part of the Spirit, was Slowly Conditioning their cores down to the next number…

It wasn't long they found those people, that the others humans were sadden to leave behind. They studied their routines and how the Self-Centered Love part of the Spirit was Conditioning them, with one soft intro to another. These soft intros were conditioning these humans, to volunteeringly destroy themselves and justifying it…

Once they grasped the core strategy of the Self-Centered Love part of the Spirit, the first male and female humans hugged each other and began to weep.

The first male and female humans then asked the Unconditional Love part of the Spirit, could they go find that human they saw in the future and talk to him? BAM. They were there before, they even heard the answer. That human was aware of them there. It's like that human was expecting them. This was a weird, but cool feeling to experience as a couple…

To break the silence that human from the "future" said "**what's up?**" "**Howse my homies doing?**"

They all busted out laughing. The first male and female humans said, "That there actually in the Abyss this time, versus looking in the door window."

The human said, "I Know." They looked confused. That human continued, "I've been observing all of you and writing it down, into a book."

Now they were really confused. "How can you do that?"

"I'm one of those creation who has not yet been physically created yet. I'm so much into watching, what's happening in this Creative Making Journey together. That when I'm physically created; I can write it down in a book for the those, being physically created in the Final Phase. This will help them understand better. From all of the "believable" lies they were conditioned to believe; to the point they loss who they were, and why we embarked on this Creative Making Journey together. All of the explanations that they were believing in; were endless loops of whatever, with intangible proposes."

With that, the human from the future hugged them. At first this was strange, but they soon received it. That human from future, knew they were about to quickly disappear. Looked at them and said, "**Good bye! See you soon.** Look me up anytime you want!"

And without thinking, they were instantly all back at the door of the Abyss. Entered through and shut it. Looking at the Unconditional Love part of the Spirit and said, "Thank YOU!"

The Unconditional Love part of the Spirit said; you can go anywhere you two, want to go. You two just have to be in agreement, while in the Abyss. If for any reason you are not in agreement; then both of you will go back to the door of the Abyss, instantly. The door will open. The Abyss will push you out and shut the door.

"Wow… Interesting and that Makes Sense. It's the same theme from opening the door together, to go in and to leave. Ok." Said the first male and female humans.

It was priceless; they couldn't have guessed all what they witness, even in a million+ years. The time it saved and understanding exactly how to save these deceived people, was priceless 2.0. They *looked deep into* the Unconditional Love part of the Spirit's Core and said, "Thank You... Thank You...Thank You!"

Silence...

They all busted out humming their forever loved music sounds.

As All of creation was humming together; the first male and female humans looked at the Unconditional Love part of the Spirit, and were talking to each other in thoughts. So that they wouldn't distract All of creation, from their beautiful humming moment together.

The first male and female humans asked the Unconditional Love part of the Spirit, was there anything else they needed to know about the Abyss? The Unconditional Love part of the Spirit said, No...

Then turned back to humming with everyone, with smiles on their faces. Taking turns hugging their generations after them...

Having this satisfaction of growing together; in this moment of their Creative Making Journey, they were getting around to head back to their abodes.

The Unconditional Love part of the Spirit spoke up and said, "There's One More!"

All of creation and the humans go, "**HUH?**" "You just said there was nothing more to know." ...

The Unconditional Love part of the Spirit continues, "I left the BEST for last. Let Me show you over here."

The first male and female humans lead them all. At first, it looked like they were All going back to the door of the Abyss. But the Unconditional Love part of the Spirit went right past it, like it didn't even exist.

Now the first male and female humans; had a more curious then ever looks on their faces, and continued with a pep in their steps.

"**A little bit farther...**

"Ok. Here we are." The Unconditional Love part of the Spirit said...

The tree was Magnificent. Those who cores were holding onto their 10s, could see somewhat of translucent glow to it... The biggest question on their faces was, why didn't we notice this before?

Hearing their thoughts, "This tree will give you an overall gentle indicator, where we are in our Creative Making Journey together...

They were still curious, but it had a like SO? Feeling to it.

"The more we get closer to Physically Eternalizing All of Creation, the tree will illuminate even more. To the point it will completely disappear...

Now they were all in on this conversation, "What is this tree's name?" Looking over to the opposite direction, "That Tree is the Door to the Abyss. What is this one? .... **WAIT A MINUTE**, Is this your tree to the Unconditional Love part of the Spirit?" ...

The Unconditional Love part of the Spirit had a **BIG Smile**.

"That's Why it Glows as we get closer to being Physically Eternalized! It's You getting excited, that Your getting closer to having Your friends, "US" being Physically Eternalized!" The first male and female humans were pumped; in this baby step moment of discovery, with All of creation and the Unconditional Love part of the Spirit.

The Unconditional Love part of the Spirit said, "**Bingo!** ...

Silence to let this overseen discovery, sink into their cores. They were so excited to be physical created, that they didn't pay attention to this Tree. They were connecting with All of creation like little children, only being fascinated with the things that stick out…

Now that they have enter the adult and being friends' stage; they were paying closer attention, to more of the details and how things work.

"This tree's name is ... *The Tree of Life* ...

The Unconditional Love part of the Spirit pauses; while remembering all of eons before, of its loneliness. Wanting to have physical friends, but settled for thought friends. And NOW eons later, actually enjoying and being with those thoughts as Physical Friends…

All of creation was observing; and soberly enjoying with the Unconditional Love part of the Spirit's, in its reflection moment.

Now they can clearly see why the Unconditional Love part of the Spirit; waited until now to show them this *Tree of Life*. **It wasn't all about the *Tree of Life*...** *It was about their friendship with each other.*

The **Unconditional Love** part of the Spirit said to the first male and female humans, "Go over to the tree and hug the tree while holding each other hands together…

The first male and female humans did just that. They were getting so accustom to doing these activities together; they did it naturally versus being apprehensive, like in the beginning.

As they were hugging the *Tree of Life*, the Tree started to glow more. Gently more and more. The first male and female humans were feeling it. They went from gently holding hands, to firmly holding hands...

When they relaxed, they started glowing themselves. The Tree and they; were now translucent to All of creation watching, and enjoying the moment with them.

"This Tree works like the other one. It only responds to male and female companions, who are in the same Unconditional Love agreement and mindset. The Tree will not start to glow, until these conditions are meant first... When the Tree starts to glow look inside the tree. It will show and tell you whatever you need to see and know. This will also be a tool for you, to help you persevere going through this Creative Making Journey together...

The first male and female humans had a surreal and temporary reference sensations they had, when they were first physically created. Looking together into the Tree and seeing the Unconditional Love part of the Spirit; in the beginning by itself, with the Self-Centered Love part of the Spirit. They peacefully went through witnessing the beginning, and up to them holding hands and hugging the Tree of Life together...

It felt like hours, but it was only a few minutes. They took a break. Turning around and smiling at the Unconditional Love part of the Spirit, for giving them this personal insight experience together...

Then looked at their families and All of creation watching them. They All appeared to be experiencing, what the first male and first female humans were experiencing. The first male and female humans asked them to verify the looks on their faces, "Did you just see what we did?" ...

Peaceful surreal smiles; with All of their cores completely on 10s said, "YES! And it was AMAZING!"

This baby step moment together, made their relationships that much more enriching. Sharing the Beginning of the Creative Making Journey together, now physically with their families and friends.

The first male and female humans looking deep into each other's eyes; while reaching out to hold each other's hands, looked into the Tree of Life again…

This time they were curious to see, what the Unconditional Love created out beyond their Earth. They were intrigued, surprised and bewildered at the same time…

They saw more humans; all of the same creation that was on their Earth, plus other species they never saw before. Period. BUT, they "looked" more advanced? In their communities and populations. How can this be, if they were the first…

They stopped looking into the Tree of Life; and turned around to the Unconditional Love part of the Spirit, "How can this be?"

The Unconditional Love part of the Spirit in a soft tone said, "All of that Creation I created, did not suffer of the blunt of releasing the Self-Centered Love part of the Spirit… Earth is ground zero. If the Self-Centered Love part of the Spirit can destroy All of Earth and its Creation; then everything else that I created, will be destroyed instantly. Poof! Gone in a twinkling of an eye…

"All that will be left is Me and the Self-Centered Love part of the Spirit…

The first male and female human's eyes were wide open, as far as they could open them.

"Now the good news! the Unconditional Love part of the Spirit said with a smirk…

ETERNALIZING CREATION FINAL PHASE

"All of those creation that you saw inside the *Tree of Life*, you can go visit and talk with them anytime. They are fully aware what's going-on on Earth, all the time. You can engage in enriching friendships with them; like you have here on Earth, with All of creation. They will and want to assist you anytime, you need "outside" help. **But will never** force themselves on you, to control you. It will be a pure friendship. A helping each other out relationship...

"If you request help; they ask you when, where and what and patiently wait until then." The Unconditional Love part of the Spirit, went silent to give them time to absorb this.

All of them; were like wow, this is deep. **How deep** is the need to persevere going get? Just as it was; just a little while ago without experiencing preserving, for the first time. They were getting flash back feelings, but ten times worse.

"Their primary assistance is going to be; to help you against the creatures, that the Self-Centered Love part of the Spirit created. The Self-Centered Love part of the Spirit's strategy is; creating creatures out away from Earth, so that you are not aware of them. They can strike you at your weakest moments, in our Creative Making Journey together...

"Throughout this Creative Making Journey together notice from time to time, there will be some strange monuments built throughout the Earth. These are reference points of who and where the Self-Centered Love part of the Spirit's created creatures came from. Go to the *Tree of Life* like you are now, and ask where these symbols came from. The creatures I created; will show you where they came from, and how to deal with those creatures...

"I know this is deep and you were not expecting, to be experiencing this right now...

"Let's go over to the door window of the Abyss; and see what the Self-Centered Love part of the Spirit is working on right now, with those humans that did not leave with the others...

The first male and female humans more intrigued than ever, ran over to the door of the Abyss.

The Unconditional Love part of the Spirit was ALL SMILES. It was like seeing a child run for the very first time, after learning how to walk. Priceless.

They looked into the window of the door of the Abyss; and instantly was taken to the view in real time, to what the Self-Centered Love part of the Spirit was soft introing to the humans. They studied the movements and symbolisms. The first female human was studying the details and the first male human was studying the overall patterns...

They turned and smiled at each other. Then hauled their rearends back over to the *Tree of Life*.

The Unconditional Love part of the Spirit *busted out laughing* with pure excitement, in how their friendship was an engaged two-way relationship.

The first male and female humans, wasted no time. They found the creation the Unconditional Love part of the Spirit created, out into the expanse beyond earth. Those humans were excited to be finally interacting with the humans from Earth. They were all respectively talking to each other, like they were best friends *for a real Long Time...*

Those humans showed them; the whats, whys, wheres, whens and the hows of those creatures the Self-Centered Love part of the Spirit created. And how to dismantle their efforts in destroying the Earth...

The first male and female humans were amazed and blown away at the same time, on how much those humans already knew. In comparison they felt like little babies, just being born from their mother's womb. Clueless but wanting to connect; in this new physical world, even all the more.

The Unconditional Love part of the Spirit's sensations were at an all time high; in seeing all the physical friends that it created, interconnecting in two-way friendships and relationships.

Those humans and the first male and female humans understood each part; in this first intervention of dismantling the Self-Centered Love part of the Spirit's strategy, in attempting to destroy All of Creation...

They took a break. Those humans introduced their families and friends to them. Sat down to have meal; made up of the unique fruits that they had, that were not on the Earth...

It was a treat to remember...

As that moment gently faded away; they found themselves on Earth with All of Creation humming once again, their favorite musical sounds...

This time; added intermittently the sounds from those new created worlds, from beyond the Earth...

After awhile the first male and female humans; once again asked the Unconditional Love part of the Spirit, "Is there anything else we need to know about the Tree of Life?"

The Unconditional Love part of the Spirit was quiet; and then in a soberly soft firm tone, "There will be times you will not be able to access the Tree of Life. This will frustrate you big time. You will begin to question yourselves, what is real and not real. Ironically; this will help you in the Final Phase, of our Creative Making Journey together...

"This will in turn, deepen your senses and the meaning of these five words. To the point, you will not need the door window to the Abyss and the Tree of Life...

"Everything that is inside of you; and the companionship you have with each other, **will be** MORE THAN ENOUGH. *For within you is the Tree of Life.*" ... "My Unconditional Love part of the Spirit...

"Our friendship with each other, is personal and unique. Enjoying this Creative Making Journey together; now and throughout all of eternity, as physical friends."

The first male and female humans; were once again in awe of their surreal moment, they just share together with All of Creation and the Unconditional Love part of the Spirit...

All of Creation with them; *Realizing* that they can do whatever is necessary, to protect their loved ones. And get them all through this Phase, to the Final Phase and beyond **TOGETHER**.

After taking a good long break with each other; their families and All of Creation. They went to work in trying to save those humans; that were entranced, by the Self-Centered Love part of the Spirit's created creatures.

After a few efforts of successfully saving just over half of those humans; entranced by the Self-Centered Love part of the Spirit's created creatures. The Self-Centered Love part of the Spirit was realizing; what the first male and female humans, other humans and All of Creation was doing to its plans.

Hmmmm.... How can I be more-subtler, so that they can't see what I'm doing. Thought the Self-Centered Love part of the Spirit...

I need to focus on hijacking their child bearing process so; that I can take over the human species, and or at least control and mislead them.

After a few generations; the Self-Centered Love part of the Spirit had entered into enough fetuses, that it was able to build a few "families" of purely Self-Centered Love part of the Spirit created human species.

Now the Self-Centered Love part of the Spirit; turned its attention away from impressing the human species with its creatures from beyond the Earth, to reasoning with the human species...

The more populated the Earth gets with humans; the more the need for humans to be organized in building, maintaining infrastructures and settling disputes...

The Self-Centered Love part of the Spirit, did soft intros throughout the next few generations. Trying to infiltrate different family linages, to insight hatred to one another...

And with a few more generations... woooohooo!

Most of the populations; was agreeing to having centralized groups of "humans," overseeing the affairs of all humans. What was best for "humanity," what was the plans and how they were going to get there...

At this point; most of the human's cores were at 2s to 4s ***and didn't*** realize they gave up their Creative Making Journey, together with the Unconditional Love part of the Spirit.

The Self-Centered Love part of the Spirit's hijacked human's cores, were always on number 1s and 2s.

Some human's cores, that were on 5s to 7s intermittently. Could sense; have premonitions and get glimpses, of what was really happening behind the scenes.

These cycles went on and on; through out Phase Three and into the beginning of Phase Four, as a carry over. Along the way, there would be near mass extinctions and annihilations of All of Creation.

Just before these near mass extinctions were about to go all in; the creation that the Unconditional Love part of the Spirit created beyond Earth, would help and intervene. On behalf of the humans and All of creation. This too helped strengthen their perseverance; in pushing forward to understanding these five words, with All of physical creation in their Creative Making Journey together.

The first time this happen, it angered the Self-Centered Love part of the Spirit to its Core. The Self-Centered Love part of the Spirit had to change its strategy yet again. It was so close to being at peace again, without created thoughts. Being infuriated it instructed all of the creatures it created beyond the Earth; to wage war against all of the creation, that was created by the Unconditional Love part of the Spirit beyond Earth...

Then the Self-Centered Love part of the Spirit; went into writing "language" into scripts and books, to create the sense of "validity" of the human's past and future events. Since the Self-Centered Love part of the Spirt is Self-Centered, it didn't have anytime to justify having emotional friendships. Its intent was to deceived and mass destroy, as soon as possible...

The humans that it was able to hijack and use their bodies, was the ones that wrote the books. They/It had no emotional feelings. So it made it easier for them to write the books/artifacts, from a human's perspective.

Note: This was when the Self-Centered Love part of the Spirit had several generations; of accumulated experience of hijacking the human fetuses, through its isolated group of humans.

The Self-Centered Love part of the Spirit made sure there were different books and "artifacts" in different parts of the Earth, to appear as though they must be legit. When the humans core numbers are in the 1s to 5s; they would tend to believe them due to the "unquestionable" details. Humans with higher core numbers would be able to find flaws, within the content.

After the Self-Centered Love part of the Spirit upgraded its strategy; to include the creatures it created beyond the Earth, into annihilating All of the creation the Unconditional Love part of the Spirit created beyond the Earth. For the purpose of *distracting the humans* from the Self-Centered Love part of the Spirit, trying to destroy Earth's Creation...

It added; *changing the narrative* it was promoting to deceive the humans, between extinctions. Once one narrative wasn't working anymore, then it would soft intro to a new narrative. It was like a list of evolutionary narratives...

Eventually going into the tipping point of Phase Four; all the narratives that the Self-Centered Love part of the Spirit tried, had no effects on the humans. Its conditioning that once worked in the beginning; was actually building up an immunity to them, within the human's CORES.

The Unconditional Love part of the Spirit's Core in creating physical eternal friends; were intentionally created with emotional sensations, to make their friendship more enriching with each other and with the Unconditional Love part of the Spirit...

This type of relationship ***doesn't*** require; books, artifacts, "mentors" and narratives to maintain it. This type of relationship feeds and grows on its own. As long as the creation desires to connect to the Unconditional Love part of the Spirit; in allowing the Unconditional Love part of the Spirit flow, within them and their love ones. Period.

Once the Self-Centered Love part of the Spirit realized this too;

it would use this to promote its "factual" reference books and "artifacts" as fact, versus basing the past on human emotions.

After All of the Creation beyond the Earth that the Unconditional Love part of the Spirit created; suffered random sporadic attacks, by the created creatures of the Self-Centered Love part of the Spirit. They All came together and Created an Unconditional Love Barrier/Shield. It was thick, strong and invisible. All of Creation that was created by the Unconditional Love part of the Spirit, could exit and enter the shield freely...

All of the creatures that the Self-Centered Love part of the Spirit created, cannot enter and exit the shield. Due to the Self-Centered Love part of the Spirit, in the creatures it created...

This was devastating to the Self-Centered Love part of the Spirit. Everything that it had put in place; to destroy All of Creation suffered a HUGE blow and wasn't recoverable...

The Self-Centered Love part of the Spirit started to panic; as All of Creation that the Unconditional Love part of the Spirit created, were going into Phase Four... of their Creative Making Journey together...

This is when humans realized; all they have to do is allow the density of the Unconditional Love part of the Spirit, to grow within their cores. As the Unconditional Love density grows in their cores; their numbers started to self-heal, up to the next number. As their numbers went up, their senses were becoming more aware of their surroundings. As the humans got to tipping point in Phase Four; they started getting addicted to restoring their senses. So that they can interact and have deeper enriching experiences, with All of Creation...

Plus; this was having a neutralizing effect, on the Self-Centered Love part of the Spirit. The Self-Centered Love part of the Spirit was slowly sliding into more depression, as the humans' cores were rising in numbers...

Why was this? The Self-Centered Love part of the Spirit was able to destroy creation, because of the fear it was able to create within the humans. When the density of the Unconditional Love was growing in their cores, that fear started to melt away...

As it was in the beginning; when the first male and female humans released, the Self-Centered Love part of the Spirit from its Abyss. Most of creation; ignored the Self-Centered Love part of the Spirit and their senses wasn't affected as much. Most of creation is on 9s and 10s that are vibrating, throughout Phases Three and Four. They can see those yet to be physically created and those who have transitioned on. Plus; all of the detailed colors, smells, hearing, tastes and touches.

As the density of the Unconditional Love part of the Spirit mutually grows within All of Creation, the Self-Centered Love part of the Spirit automatically contracts. Just like in the beginning; when the Unconditional Love part of the Spirit was creating all of its thought friends. As it created them; the Self-Centered Love part of the Spirit had to contract, to make room for them.

Note: The individual created thought's physically body is unique to its spirit. If the spirit transitions on from its body during Phase Three and Four; then when the spirit takes back on its physical body in Phase Five, it will have the same body it had when the body was first physically created.

Note: To clarify. The body is in same shape of the spirit. The spirit is in the same shape of the body. This is the same for ALL of **Creation. *All have the same value*.** From the dirt, smallest of molecules of species, trees, grasses, rocks, crystals, liquids, creatures, etc.; their physical shapes are all in the same shape as their spirits.

Note: All of the creation that the Self-Centered Love part of the Spirit creates, are one-timers. They never had a previous spirit. The body is created one time, and is filled with the "soul" of which is the Self-Centered Love part of the Spirit. When its creation transitions on, the soul returns back to the Self-Centered Love part of the Spirit. The body deteriorates back into the Self-Centered Love part of the Spirit...

If the Self-Centered Love part of the Spirit hijacks the fetus of the Unconditional Love part of the Spirit's creation; when its "soul" leaves that body, that body will go through the deteriorating process. And be reabsorbed back into creation during Phase Three and Four.

Note: There is no transitioning on during Phase Five and beyond. All of Creation is Physically Eternalized, and having physically created offspring when they desire to. Each enjoying the Child, Adult, Friend, Companion and Parent cycles.

Note: Eternal Companions decided who they wanted to be a companion with, in the beginning when first were created thoughts. This allows them to Enjoy the whole Creative Making Journey together. At times "appear" separated.

Note: All of Creation always had and always will have access to the "Garden" part of the Earth, even in the last Phase Five and throughout all eternity...

Note: It was the Self-Centered Love part of the Spirit's narrative; that the first male and female humans were banished, from the "Garden" ...

They were NEVER was banished.

Note: The Technology "appears" to be more advance beyond Earth. Technology is same everywhere throughout all creation. Each is unique to each location and used more in different areas. Technology only was created; to make up for the short falls of

Humans with Core Numbers below 10, and Creation is suffering the consequences of it…

All of creation agreed to the releasing of the Self-Centered Love part of the Spirit from its Abyss.

Here are two charts to better breakdown the five characteristics of Unconditional Love and Self-Centered Love parts of the Spirit.

THE SPIRIT: When Creating Physical Friends			
50% Unconditional Love		**50% Self-Centered Love**	
5 CHARACTERISTICS	CORE:	5 CHARACTERISTICS	CORE:
Eyes: Insight	Faith	Nosight	Panic
Hearing: Accountability	Perseverance	Uncommitted	Anger
Taste: Love	Compassion	Hatred	Revenge
Touch: Extrovert	Forgiveness	Introvert	Anxiety
Smell: Teaching	Peace	Doubt	Depression
NOTE: The Core of Faith is Insight, The Core of Perseverance is Accountably, The Core of Compassion is Love, The Core of Forgiveness is Extrovert, The Core of Peace is Teaching.		NOTE: The Core of Panic is Nosight, The Core of Anger is Uncommitted, The Core of Revenge is Hatred, The Core of Anxiety is Introvert, The Core of Depression is Doubt.	

THE SPIRIT: Friends Physically Eternal	
100% Unconditional Love	
5 CHARACTERISTICS	CORE:
Insight	Faith
Accountability	Perseverance
Love	Compassion
Extrovert	Forgiveness
Teaching	Peace

NOTE: The Core of Faith is Insight, The Core of Perseverance is Accountably, The Core of Compassion is Love, The Core of Forgiveness is Extrovert, The Core of Peace is Teaching.

Unconditional Love is Appreciated the Most
When it is Lost.

Why is That?

DEBUNKING THE TOP TEN

When we allow Unconditional Love part of the Spirit to penetrate, permeate, saturate, restore our senses and flourish in, with, through, around and beyond our Spirits, Minds and Bodys; we automatically have the fullness of being completely satisfied, totally at peace with all of creation and lack nothing. Twenty-four seven for ever and ever.

This list of the supposed traditional ten commandments; have been twisted by the Self-Centered Love part of the Spirit, out of desperation to increase its odds in prolonging its own life…

The Self-Centered Love part of the Spirit twisted what are the top ten strategies of the Self-Centered Love part of the Spirit; into a list of condemning, intimidating and putting fear into creation. To the point it caused humans; to feel like they had/have to submit to "authority", by observing rituals that make them temporarily "holy" for a brief moment. And then repeat the process hourly, daily, weekly, monthly, yearly, etc. The Perfect Bondage, by fear of being out of the "grace" of a "god – an ascended being."

Here is/are the Top Ten Cloaked Strategies, of the Self-Centered Love part of the Spirit.

One: Self-Centered Love, Loves to Covet. *Twisted to*: Do Not Covet.

Two: Self-Centered Love, Loves to Lie. *Twisted to*: Do Not Lie.

Three: Self-Centered Love, Loves to Steal. *Twisted to*: Do Not Steal.

Four: Self-Centered Love, Loves to Kill. *Twisted to*: Do not Kill.

Five: Self-Centered Love, Loves to Make Idols of "Ascended Beings." *Twisted to*: Do not Make Idols.

Six: Self-Centered Love, Loves to Worship Itself. *Twisted to*: Do not Have Any Other "gods".

Seven: Self-Centered Love, Loves to Create False Witnesses. *Twisted to*: Do not Bear False Witness.

Eight: Self-Centered Love is Worthless. *Twisted to*: Do not Take the Name of your "god" in vain.

Nine: Self-Centered Love, Loves to Destroy Families. *Twisted to*: Honor your mother and father.

Ten: Self-Centered Love, Loves to Create Debt Slavery. *Twisted to*: Remember the Sabbath Day.

Now let's list them all together.

The Top Ten Strategies of Self-Centered Love: Covets, Lies, Steals, Kills, Makes Idols, Worships Itself, Creates False Witnesses, Makes Creation Worthless, Destroys Families and Creates Debt Slavery.

HOW GOLDEN IS THE GOLDEN RULE?

So, in everything, do to others what you would have them do to you, for this sums up the law and the prophets. Matthew 7:12. NIV

Unconditional Love part of the Spirit; Automatically does this with all of creation without even thinking about it, so that all of creation is nourishing and flourishing in Unconditional Love together.

Self-Centered Love part of the Spirit justifies, "I love destroying creation so I will destroy creation. "I love confrontations / chaos / sacrifices / fear mongering / central governing / death / lies /; so, I will create confrontations / chaos / sacrifices / fear mongering / fascism / death / lies to others.

Unconditional Love is Appreciated the Most
When it is Lost.

Why is That?

FINAL PHASE

PHASE FOUR

When you base a story on time, events and places, it becomes impersonal to the point it loses validity.

When you base a story on never ending endless loops; of random learning experiences in trying to "ascend," it becomes disheartening for the masses while just a few "feel" like they've "ascended." Let alone, it diminishes the value of the unique individual creature and all of creation at large.

When a journey is based on emotionally connecting, it personally becomes an enriching life relationship. When one's passion is wanting to manifest it with all of creation; to become a part of the whole journey, it makes one's life journey even more enriching…

The only way we can truly connect emotionally is understanding what Unconditional and Self-Centered Love really are. Then make the choice for either side.

All other narratives are self-centered, distant and cold.

PHASE FOUR THEME:
COMPANION MINDSET AND DEVELOPMENT.

As far as our eyes can see the majesty of creation. Our ears hear of her stories of long ago. There is no greater story then this, The

SPIRIT who makes room in its life. So that It can create friends like us; to share with all of creation ALL of eternity together, as friends and family in Unconditional Love forever and ever.

FINAL PHASE: CHAPTER ONE

Note: These Chapter Numbers are References to the Content Associated with PHASE FOUR. AKA The Final Phase.

Self-Centered Love part of the Spirit's narrative is: They will beat their weapons into plows and pruning hooks, to control creations focus on itself.

The Unconditional Love part of the Spirit with All of Creation is **ALL into**; Restoring All of Creation's senses to deepen their relationships, with each other and the Unconditional Love part of the Spirit…

Together they will undo what the Self-Centered Love part of the Spirit did; in an attempt to mess up and destroy All of creation. While Restoring All of Creation into its original harmonious state of being. Now knowing the meaning of these five words: faith, perseverance, compassion, forgiveness and peace.

Self-Centered Love part of the Spirit's narrative is: I believe in the things I don't see, more than the things I can see.

The Unconditional Love part of the Spirit: I believe more in Unconditional Love part of the Spirit then I do Self-Centered Love part of the Spirit.

If **Unconditional Love** is an abstract concept in one's mind? Then start this journey in restoring our senses by; allowing Unconditional Love to be in, with, through, around and beyond our spirit, mind and body. By having an Unconditional Love friendship with a dog, that is full of unconditional love...

Dogs' sensitivity to one's spirit, mental condition and body is phenomenal. They Know when to: cheer us up; help us move forward and have the perfect timing on comforting us. ALL second to none.

While Moving into the beginning of establishing the Final Phase; the anticipation of "Aliens" will appear in our everyday lives, of those who are physically created. To the extreme point, of some fearing an alien invasion. Aliens taking over the world; being slaves to. Again, this is based on fear...

The Self-Centered Love part of the Spirit will try establish an "Alien" invasion narrative, in hopes the masses will focus on that. Versus allowing the Unconditional Love part of the Spirit to manifest: in, with, through, around and beyond our spirits, minds and bodys...

For those humans that allow their cores to number up towards 9s and 10s; they will begin to see and interact with those, that are yet to be physically created and those who have transitioned on. Those who have transitioned on; will become more proactive in working with the humans that cores are on 9s and 10s. Because they'll both be convinced, they can see and touch each other...

How can those who have transitioned on be mistreated again? And *now they can* follow through with *protecting* their physically created friends. Who can stop them? No one.

Now what was backwards. The Self-Centered Love part of the Spirit's creatures were living longer lives than the Unconditional Love part of the Spirit's creatures. Due to the Self-Centered Love part of the Spirit. During this Phase Four this gets flipped backwards. As the humans/creation allow their cores to number up, the longer their lives will be...

Another way of saying it. The Unconditional Love part of the Spirit's creation pursuing Unconditional Love, will be automatically living longer lives. The creation that insists on hanging onto being Self-Centered, will automatically live shorter lives. This too gets back into balance.

Examples: The transitioned-on elephants; will be saving those physically created elephants, that are being poached. Elephants will no longer be at the mercy; of finding an Unconditional Love part of the Spirit human, to help them escape death. Who can stop these transitioned-on elephants, helping their own kind? ...

It deepens their bond for each other even more. Their Unconditional Love family, becomes more enriching to the nth degree. As the generations get closer to the end of the Final Phase; their spirits, minds, bodys become more at peace, with no fears of being hunted.

Other animals will come to their rescue as well. Pit bulls, jaguars, tigers, rams, bulls, kangaroos, etc. Who can stop them? It's the perfect solution to putting every thing back into balance; to eliminate that "the strong survive" lie, that the Self-Centered Love part of the Spirit would brain wash creation with. It's a brilliant way to balance out the life experiences, from the beginning to the end of the Final Phase.

FINAL PHASE: CHAPTER TWO

You can take All of Creation out of the Garden of Earth; but you can't take the Garden of Earth, out of All of Creation.

The Garden of Earth is the Center of Earth. The Earth is in the Center of Creation.

The Artisan Wells of Unconditional Love held the canopy over and around the Earth up in place.

In Unconditional Love there is no darkness, night and or shadows. When the Self-Centered Love part of the Spirit was released into creation, then there was darkness.

The volume of information in traditional narratives, rituals, prophecies, rules and regulations; do not automatically validate that they are real, and the truth. They come across more as condemnation; not worthy of and the fear of being rejected, regardless. Most of this is the Self-Centered Love part of the Spirit justifying itself, as having a valid place in All of Creation.

The truth about the Unconditional Love part of the Spirit is in All of Its Creation, regardless of how perverted it becomes by Self-Centered Love part of the Spirit...

A single male and female; in an Unconditional Love relationship with each other, creates the desire to reproduce. To celebrate who they are; and the relationship that they have together, with zero Self-Centered Love.

Why is there so much energy being put into leaving; and or hoping someone will come along, to fix everything?

It's time for letting the Unconditional Love part of the Spirit saturate us to the point; of becoming one in the spirit, one in the mind and one in the body, as Friends with Unconditional Love in driven passion.

Just as the first male and female humans released the Self-Centered Love part of the Spirit, into all creation. Now the time has come; for All of Creation to release the Self-Centered Love part of the Spirit from our lives, to return back to its Abyss.

This Final Phase is only activated, when a human(s) is(are) ready in their Core(s) to activate it. Once activated, the human(s) and creation are to be dedicated to the very end. So that All of Creation is restored; as in the Days of the Garden Earth, before the Self-Centered Love part of the Spirit was released...

The best time to activate this; is when the meaning of the five words is understood and harnessed. Harnessing the meaning of these five words; will help All of Creation navigate through this releasing of the Self-Centered Love part of the Spirit from All of Creation, to go back to its Abyss.

As this is set in motion; All of Creation will begin to see and will become normal seeing, the lion laying down beside and being at peace with the lamb.

All of Creation will begin to see; and become normal seeing, those living by the Unconditional Love and those by Self-Centered Love.

In perfect Unconditional Love there is no centralized groups, trying to monitor and control Creation.

If a human transitions on before 100 years old, they will be considered a child. *Highlighting* the deprogramming of the human's core; from the narrative that the Self-Centered Love part of the Spirit, was planting in the Cores of All of Creation.

The Self-Centered Love part of the Spirit **had to be released;** to understand the five words and deepen their relationship, with the Unconditional Love part of the Spirit.

Once humans and All of Creation embark on this Final Phase; and accomplish putting 100% of the Self-Centered Love part of the Spirit back into Its Abyss, then Unconditional Love will be in All, with All and Through All.

Self-Centered Love part of the Spirit's narrative is, the word was made flesh. Unconditional Love part of the Spirit Manifested Physical Touch; to Make Creation Balanced, Complete and Perfectly Satisfied.

Whatever a human thinks in their Core, so shall they gravitate to it.

Our Decision is Our Foundation.

The narrative of the Self-Centered Love part of the Spirit is; in the beginning, I knew you before you were in your mother's womb.

The Unconditional Love part of the Spirit; loves All of Creation so much, that it allowed us to choose the time and location we wanted to be physically created.

The narrative of the Self-Centered Love part of the Spirit is, in the last days I will pour out My Spirit on all flesh.

The Unconditional Love part of the Spirit will restore All of Creation, whenever All of Creation is ready to be restored.

Automatically; when the Creation *releases* the Self-Centered Love part of the Spirit, from their Cores.

The narrative of the Self-Centered Love part of the Spirit is; Faith the size of a mustard seed, can move mountains.

Unconditional Love part of the Spirit as small as a mustard seed, can move a mountain of Self-Centered Love.

The narrative of the Self-Centered Love part of the Spirit is, Greater than He that is in me, than he that is in the world.

The Unconditional Love part of the Spirit is greater in my core, than the Self-Centered Love part of the Spirit in the world.

As the Unconditional Love part of the Spirit grows; the Self-Centered Love part of the Spirit contracts, back to Its Abyss. All of Creation with higher core numbers, will be able to see this in real time and motion.

Tarot, Physics, Dowsing, etc: For the most part have been good. Those that are being used by the Self-Centered Love part of the Spirit; are doing so in a way, to give the good one's bad names…

The one's that quiet themselves, and tune into the Spirit at a deeper level. Their cores are on the high side, 7s to 8s. As religion starts unraveling; those followers will gravitate towards the Tarot Readers, Physics and Dowsing, to get a better perception of their current conditions…

As the density of their cores heighten, the lesser need in tarot readers, physics and dowsing. Their restoring cores; will automatically restore their senses. These will help them understand clearly their condition; and how to personally navigate, through their own challenges and life.

FINAL PHASE: CHAPTER THREE
FOCUSES ON TRENDS

100% Owned: Employee Organizations. This eliminates the narrative; of there must be an "isolated governing group," to operate the organization. Pro-active employees know what's the best way; on how to run the organization, in the most efficient and productive ways. While reducing tons of overhead costs… TONS.

Free Energy: Energy naturally abounds in All of Creation. It's just learning/relearning how to harness it; to acquire and ethically use it, for the good for all.

Note: Towards the end of this Final Phase, it will become less and less necessary to. When All of Creation's Core numbers move back to 10 and the 9s. The spirit, mind and body become more satisfied; without having the need for "necessities" as supplements, to make up for the lower core numbers.

John Ellis Water: As nicked named, will put water back to its Original Created Bond Memory. This was brilliant observation by John Ellis; in developing a water distillation process, that naturally puts water back in its original created bond sequence…

When the Self-Centered Love part of the Spirit was released into all of Creation; its intent is to destroy Creation's natural flow of living, with each other…

Water being on the top of the list; due to how it flows in, with, through, around and beyond All of Creation...

When water is returned to its original created bond pattern; it automatically restores, the other water source's distorted bonds...

Example: A pond of water, with the distorted water bond patterns. Put in a big tank of John Ellis distilled water; and it will restore the whole pond of distorted water, back to its original bond pattern.

The Self-Centered Love part of the Spirit's creatures can't tolerate the Original Bond Water; so, they either die and or leaves the pond...

Example: A water well has the distorted water bond patterns, and is a cesspool of Self-Centered Love part of the Spirit's creatures. Pour in a big bucket of John Ellis distilled water; into the water well and it will change all of the distorted water bonds, back to their original created bonds. The water well becomes good to use again, as a fresh water source.

Note: Always double check the water first before drinking it.

As the water's created bond is restored; ***it will assist*** in restoring, All of Creation to its Original State of Physical Existence...

ZERO: The Self-Centered Love part of the Spirit's narratives; that All of Creation "must" have: governments, "certain" medicines, people to administer the "certain" medicines, mass public education centers, worshipping certain "entities", only designated areas for worshipping certain "entities", Endless loops of trying to understand what life is, urban free roaming camps, "controlled" waste and water disposal systems, etc.

Humans Stop Wearing Facial Makeup: They will embrace their inner beauty, more than their "surface" beauty...

The Self-Centered Love part of the Spirit is constantly whispering in their minds, "You're not beautiful... You're not as beautiful like the others... If you wear this shade and colors, it will **enhance** your outer beauty." ... Meanwhile It loads up the different makeups, with substances that harm the humans. The human focuses on the textures and smells; and overlooks the harms, to be "more" beautiful.

Hemp Plant Products: Replaces the Wood types that the Self-Centered Love part of the Spirit narrative, sold as being "better."

Hemp Makes Stronger: Belts, shoes, framing – yes framing, etc. Bio-friendly in cleaning up toxins in ground. No mining, etc. Panels made for vehicles, appliances, etc. last longer and stronger than metal panels. Takes less water to produce and puts at least 20% more oxygen in the atmosphere.

The Stronger Wood types can take up to 50 to 100 years to grow; whereas Hemp can grow in 120 days. Done right; it can be repeatedly harvested annually, with less water and time.

The Hemp Plant also offers medicines, for those with lower core numbers. Naturally repels bad bacteria, created by the Self-Centered Love part of the Spirit.

Bamboo Plant Products: Naturally repels the bad bacteria, created by the Self-Centered Love part of the Spirit.

Bamboo Fibers Make great Clothing Items. Furniture, etc.

Body Building/Workouts: Gyms, Lifting Weights, Tread Mills, Etc., will fade away. These focus on single and or a small area of muscles. These are miss leading the human, that they are "strong" and ready to go. But in reality; this sets them up for bad injuries, that might take several months to recoup – if can. These were distractions promoted by the Self-Centered Love part of the Spirit.

Calisthenics focus on several groups of muscles, just using one's own body weight. The human starts in the areas, where they are the least flexible. Building those sets of muscles, that will make them eventually more flexible in that area. Just using their own body weight.

Those that continue with calisthenics; using just their own body weight to build muscles, will be much more "athletically" and agile then those who don't. It's impressive.

Qigong Primary Overall Health: This is a deeper focus on the real Core of the Creature; just behind the naval area for energy, strength, thought, passion and healing…

This Self-Centered Love part of the Spirit's narrative, focuses on the body as the problem.

When our Cores are in balance and in harmony with All of Creation; then the health of the body will be put back into balance, heal and etc.

The physical heart that pumps blood throughout the body; will be less taxing on the body, thus allowing the body to live longer time spans…

The body's blood plasma gets stronger, and more predominately a lighter color. To the point; it becomes more of a naturally translucent glowing energy, that flows through the body. Versus the red color blood, that the Self-Centered Love part of the Spirit's narrative has been…

Those who master this can either transition on; until the Decision Day for the Self-Centered Love part of the Spirit. Then become both a physically and spiritually eternalized body…

Or until then; choose to be a 100% restored physically creature in this current world; as the first male and female humans were in the garden, before releasing the Self-Centered Love part of the Spirit into All of Creation...

Then become an eternalized body on or just before, the Self-Centered Love part of the Spirit's Decision Day.

Thoughts: Some meditations focus on having "no" thoughts; so the body can get into a state of using that energy for healing the body, versus wasting that energy on random thoughts ...

It's 50/50. The random thoughts, most of the time is energy wasted. Having "No" thoughts meditations; do help ween the mind off random thoughts, thus justifying the "no" thought meditations...

However; the Unconditional Love part of the Spirit had thoughts of creation. And *those thoughts* of creation, **brought a more enriching life,** to the Unconditional Love part of the Spirit...

Since All of Creation is created in the likeness; of the Infinite Unconditional Love part of the Spirit, then we too can have thoughts of life...

Thoughts of Restoration in our lives; that produces Infinite ways, of expressing Unconditional Love to and with All of Creation...

What supersedes "no" thought meditations; is thoughts that produce life in, with, through, around and beyond our lives. To the point, they become physically created. Just like the Unconditional Love part of the Spirit, did with us – with All of Creation...

We are in the Likeness of the Unconditional Love part of the Spirit...

This isn't mind over matter...

This is the Unconditional Love part of the Spirit with Us; in our spirits, minds and bodys. **Creating** *restoration in our lives* **with us**.

PERIOD. *Let our spirits, minds and bodys absorb that thought...*

Examples: These can start out as thoughts during the day, replacing current mediating thoughts and or when trying to relax to go to sleep.

Note: Once we get into this routine training, it will eventually become automatic. When our thoughts of restoration start to physically manifest in our lives, it will become addictive.

OK. Now the Examples:
Visualize these in Action...

My Spirit is Getting More Intuitive.
My Spirit is Connecting with the Unconditional
Love part of Spirit in a Deeper Way.
My Spirit is Connecting with Those Who have Transitioned
On and Those Who are Yet to be Physically Created.
My Spirit Interacting with My Mind and
Body is Getting Stronger.
My Spirit's Core is Getter Stronger.
Etc.

My Mind is Getting More Intuitive.
My Mind is Connecting with the Unconditional
Love part of Spirit in a Deeper Way.
My Mind is Connecting with Those Who have Transitioned
On and Those Who are Yet to be Physically Created.
My Mind Interacting with My Spirit and
Body is Getting Stronger.
My Mind's Memory is Getting Stronger.
My Mind is Being Completely Restored.
My Mind Stamina is Getting Stronger.
My Mind is Understanding Different Concepts.
My Mind's Focus is Getting Stronger.
My Mind's Core is Getter Stronger.
Etc.

My Body Tissues are Getting More Intuitive.
My Body is Connecting with the Unconditional
Love part of Spirit in a Deeper Way.
My Body is Connecting with Those Who have Transitioned
On and Those Who are Yet to be Physically Created.
My Body Interacting with My Spirit and
Mind is Getting Stronger.
My Body is Being Completely Restored.
My Body's Stamina is Getting Stronger.
My Body's Eyesight is 20/20.
My Muscles are Growing Stronger.
My Body's Hair on My Head is Thick and Retaining its Color.
My Body's Blood Vessels are Strong and Healthy.
My Body's Core is Getter Stronger.
Etc.

My Relationship is Getting More Intuitive.
My Relationship is Connecting with the Unconditional
Love part of Spirit in a Deeper Way.
My Relationship is Connecting with Those
Who have Transitioned On and Those Who
are Yet to be Physically Created.
My Relationship Interacting with My Mind
and Body is Getting Stronger.
My Relationship with My Companion is
Getting Stronger and Stronger.
My Relationship with My Child/ren is/are Getting Stronger.
My Relationship Connecting with All of
Creation is Getting Better and Better.
My Relationship's Cores is Getting Stronger.
Etc.

Me and My Spiritmate is Getting More Intuitive.
Me and My Spiritmate is Connecting with the
Unconditional Love part of Spirit in a Deeper Way.
Me and My Spiritmate is Connecting with

Those Who have Transitioned On and Those
Who are Yet to be Physically Created.
Me and My Spiritmate Interacting with Our
Minds and Bodys is Getting Stronger.
Me and My Spiritmate is Getting Stronger and Stronger.
Me and My Spiritmate with Our Child/ren is Getting Stronger.
Me and My Spiritmate Connecting with All of
Creation is Getting Better and Better.
Me and My Spiritmate Cores are Getter Stronger.
Etc.

My Wealth is Getting Stronger and Stronger.
My Assets are Getting Stronger and Stronger.
My Incomes Streams are Getting Stronger and Stronger.
My Unconditional Love Density is
Getting Stronger and Stronger.
My Connecting with All of Creation is
Getting Stronger and Stronger.
Etc.

My Core is Getting Stronger and Stronger.

All of Creation's Senses Restored: As Creation allows the Unconditional Love part of the Spirit to nourish and flourish within them; it will be at the rate, Creation is willing to embrace the restoration of their senses.

Human Places of Abode: Humans will no longer live in cities, sub divisions, etc. They will build their abodes up in and above the trees, using framework structures made of chitin, etc. All natural substances made in Creation; that are super strong and hold a lot of weight, with zero deterioration.

This will eliminate all surface roads, dwellings and support structures...

This will Allow All of Creation to freely roam where ever they want; without being restricted, by roads and other surface level structures.

Previous "Civilization" Structures: Will be torn down and naturally put back in their original created forms. As well as the "toxic" parts of the construction components. This will allow all of those distorted created substances, to be restored and released back into Creation. Liberated to enjoy being with All of Creation, once again.

This will also create more surface areas to grow, Fruit Trees and other Food Bearing Plants.

Religion Exposed: And becomes obsolete. The Self-Centered Love part of the Spirit is addicted to its spirit form. That it has known forever in the past, present and sees no other way in the future. It's *infatuated* with itself. The Self-Centered Love part of the Spirit has no plans of competing; relinquishing to the idea, of being a part of physically created creation and spirit. Never. Period…

This is the framework that It uses; to build all different types of unique religions. Each having their own unique set of rituals, to "ascend" to a "higher" form of oneself…

They cover the full spectrum, from one side to the other. On one end, it's just pure mediation of being in the now. To the opposite end; of submitting and complying to a "holy" individual, in hopes of escaping an eternal "hell." …

Then the Self-Centered Love part of the Spirit subtly crafted each type of religion; to program each "believer" that they are eternally saved and all the other religions are wrong. These separates and pits the believers, against each other. At times; justifying they have the right to lead crusades, against the "opposing" religion…

The Self-Centered Love part of the Spirit will establish some "prophets" who prophesy; actual events that take place, to gain a following. It even goes to great distances; to have the creatures it created beyond Earth, to come to Earth to instill fear and validation…

Those who are seeking to "lead" new followers, are avoiding their own personally friendship with the Unconditional Love part of the Spirit. This too, will become obvious to all observers…

Then like an internal alarm; they'll awaken and let loose of the remaining Self-Centered Love part of the Spirit, that is within them. All creation will become addicted; to having **their own personal** friendship with the Unconditional Love part of the Spirit, that provides for All of Creation…

As the humans go through this PHASE FOUR; it will be easier to see how this is distracting them, from Allowing the Unconditional Love part of the Spirit restoring their cores to number 10s.

All of Creation Beyond Earth: As the human's core numbers are being restored from 1s to 10s; so, will the connecting increase between locations, throughout All of Creation beyond Earth. It will become easier and easier, to the point it is normal. ***Aaaaand*** Addicting…

It will have the same feel to it; like looking forward, and getting excited about having family reunions.

FINAL PHASE: CHAPTER FOUR

Once Phase Four gets past tipping point; the Self-Centered Love part of the Spirit, starts to retract and gets depressed...

While depressed; the Self-Centered Love part of the Spirit analyzes all of its attempts, and strategies in destroying all of creation...

Then concludes; the best strategy it ever had over tribes, religions, different types of central governing groups, created creatures beyond Earth, was whispering soft quiet words of "believable" doubts about themselves in the ears of humans...

For a moment, the Self-Centered Love part of the Spirit got so angry with itself. It was infuriated. It was calling itself all kinds of derogatory names. All that time and effort was wasted; in putting all of its trust in the visuals, in destroying All of Creation. When all it had to do; was focus on whispering soft quiet words of doubts, about themselves in the ears of humans. And the creation that was around them; to convince them, those words of doubts must be true? ...

The humans with Core numbers below 10, would be tempted to believe that the words must be true. Especially when the Self-Centered Love part of the Spirit would orchestrate, with the other creation surrounding that/those human(s)...

After the Self-Centered Love part of the Spirit reasoned with itself; over and over to verify its best strategy to cracking and stopping this new awakening, that All of Creation was experiencing together...

This awakening was new to All of Creation, and was in the beginning cycle of getting addicted...

FINAL PHASE: CHAPTER FIVE

The Idea That Humans are experimental, in hopes of finding a super human form of existence. All stems from the beginning; when the first male and female humans wanted to understand, the words: Faith, Perseverance, Compassion, Forgiveness and Peace...

Due to being created eternal and "perfect" in the beginning, not in a trial basis, test and the retry non-sense. The Unconditional Love part of the Spirit is perfect, and eternal upfront – *not over time.*

FINAL PHASE: CHAPTER SIX

Final Phase OV Journey Diary Samples

10-01-22 I asked Max; if he would give me a sign that he was close by, during half time while mowing the grass. When done; sat down by the fire pit, in the back yard. Then I heard the neighbor's voice, he had transitioned on about a year now. He said; Max let him know he had transition on and asked, if I would talk to you. (I would have never guessed; Max would have chosen that way to let me know, he is still close by) …

The transitioned neighbor said everyone that has transitioned on and yet to be physically created; are excited that OV has taken up the challenge, to release the Self-Centered Love part of the Spirit back into its Abyss. Where it resided before being released…

He understood if I didn't want to follow through *but emphasized*; I was the only option up to this point, that looks promising: people skills, insight and able to write it down for creation to understand it. Plus; the love for all of creation, pursuing a vegan diet to emphasize this dedication…

He apologized for the neighbors. I thanked him, for his kind words. And he departed.

Then just afterwards; a chipmunk came up to me and sat on the rocker, curved wood rocker seat. *We looked at each other for a moment. No movement.* **Peaceful.** Then it walked and ran off…

Max then said; word is getting out about the Final Phase has started and the animals want to see you for themselves, but didn't know where to find you. So, I have been showing them how to find you. I'll be bringing to you more creatures. To let you know I'm close by.

I felt at peace. This soberly confirmed to me; this is the healthy way, to emotionally detox. And the path I must take, to help stay focus on the end goal.

10-01-22 I Miss holding you Max. *Max said, me too.* The greatest thing Unconditional Love part of the Spirit ever created was physical touch. And All creation wants to experience it...

Even the Self-Centered Love part of the Spirit was and is addicted to touch; but quickly snaps out of it, and focuses on destroying the vulnerable and innocent creation.

Max, Cooper and Smudge were sharing their experiences, when they transitioned on. Very dramatic, fearful and scary. Then subsides too surreal, peaceful and beautiful...

Max expressed seeing a lot of mental and physical abusive deaths; millions by the day. Extremely traumatized and scared. He wanted to come back inside his body, but he couldn't. He felt sad and stressed at how I would see his body, without his spirit present in it. He was hoping to jump back into his body before I got back, so I wouldn't have noticed the event. *Helpless.* All the death transitioning around him. All in shock then dissipates to surreal, peace and having the freedom to navigate anywhere. He LOVED IT. But he wanted to be back here in this world, to experience the touch...

Cooper mentioned the same but not as many deaths, maybe half...

Smudge mentioned the same but hardly any deaths, like Cooper and Max...

It felt awesome working as a family, in our first two days. 10-4th and 5th-22.

10-5-22 8:30pm. Max was sharing with me; that Smudge shared with him, about my youth...

Cooper shared with him; my transitioning from single parenting, to pursuing my OV passions...

And vise-a-verse with each other; knowing more about whats it like, physically interacting with me in my life: beginning, middle, latter and now all together. What they all have in common. How they like interacting with me. All three the same. But NOW all complete individually and as a family...

Max pointed out how our Cores were matched up. Smudge was a racer (born to). I did a lot of racing with bike, boat, tubing, skiing. High pace activities...

Cooper was technical; where I focused on the technical logic of writing books, setting up distribution centers, manufacturing layouts, etc...

Max was socialite, compassionate, are you ok, let's play, take a break. That was how I was when branching out, to be me and make sure are you ok...

So it validates; it was not a coincidence, that the pattern happened the way it did. It was meant to be as proof that we were a family of created thoughts; wanting to be physically created together in our Creative Making Journey, more than ever.

This special meeting I've been hinting to the last few days, is with the Unconditional Love part of the Spirit. Along with the first male and female humans and their Pitbulls. OV will be there too. Once I made the physical commitment, all their Cores leaped for joy...

Finally, we made it. No more waiting. The first male and female humans and Unconditional Love part of the Spirit saw You (Max and Me) in the future as the ones; who started the process of releasing the Self-Centered Love part of the Spirit, back into its Abyss. Now that future moment in time; is manifesting in real time of their meeting each other, in the beginning.

The first male and female humans knew exactly what was going to happen, after the release of the Self-Centered Love part of the Spirit. It wasn't a shock. It was more of the *physically* experiencing it. So; they were able to now match the physical touch experience of it; with what they saw beforehand.

11-11-22 Max opened up to me when I was crying, for missing holding him. Max said that when he first crossed over, its immediately addictive. I was so curious, I kept checking things out. Then realized I went too far. When I couldn't come back to you. I started to cry...

OV; you always told me, that we need to stop at this or that line to give people and creatures space. And one day we won't have to; we will be free, to roam everywhere. I cried and cried OV, that I couldn't be with you physically. I miss your touch OV. Then it made sense to me; not to cross the line, so that we can be with each other all the time...

I said to Max, It's ok. You always wanted to be free and now you are. *Wiping* the tears from my eyes...

Max said, yes, but not no more. I don't want to be free anymore. I want to be with you...

I cried. I said to Max, We will again big buddy. We both now know; that crossing the line is addictive and we must be careful not to, unless we want to stay there. One day those who have transitioned on; will be able to interact with those who are physically created, in this Final Phase, as it gains momentum.

This gives me more peace Max, that you shared that with me. Knowing as well, we have to do this sooner or later. **AND IT**

MIGHT AS WELL BE NOW. *Thank you, Big Buddy!* It's an honor and privilege, to be on this journey with you. Its Priceless!

11-22-22 Getting excited to seeing creation; getting excited about coming alive in their personal friendships, with the Unconditional Love part of the Spirit

11-29-22 Moving into the embracing; doubling what the Unconditional Love Spirit manifested in the previous week, in my core and All of Creation.

12-02-22 Embracing and absorbing enough continual Unconditional Love part of the Spirit within my Core; to restore my senses, so that I can see and interact with Max, Cooper, Smudge and Betsy in this world. Say what? Yup!

01-04-23 We had just started the 17th week, since Max had transitioned on. I'm getting excited about the momentum building; as we transitioned as a family, in restoring our senses…

As I was saying this to Max, Cooper, Smudge and Betsy appeared outside my car window as I was driving home. *I began to cry.* I was naïve when I was young, leaving home (the farm) to pursue life. Betsy was my first horse…

My family showed no interest, in taking care of all the farm animals when I left. I had to make the decision to "sell" Betsy. *It tore me up.* I didn't want to do it, but I had no choice. *I had flash backs of watching her leave in the horse trailer, never to see her again.* From my self-restricted vision…

Now experiencing this with Max. Our love ones that have transitioned on; are always close by, *if we loved each other enough.*

I asked Max; how long have you known this and he said from day one, just before he was transitioning on. Along with Cooper and Smudge…

I cried all the way home. In my tears, I said to Betsy, "I'm sooo sorry the way I left you. You didn't deserve that" …

Betsy replied back, "OV; the Self-Centered Love part of the Spirit was trying to take us all out, in those days. You gave me attention, no one else ever did. Your family didn't even make an attempt to spend time with me, like you did. It was more than I had ever experienced. Thank you. **And NOW** we're together forever. *Nothing* can *ever* separate us now."

Betsy; like Cooper and Smudge had ministered to me to the point, she healed a lot of scars that I wasn't able to heal from. And now as we go into doubling the Unconditional Love part of the Spirit; to restore my senses every week mode, Betsy shows up. How fitting, and the timing is priceless. I would of never guest; that was going to be one of the manifestations, in doubling every week.

FINAL PHASE: CHAPTER SEVEN

Single parenting is the loneliest; frustrating, challenging and rewarding life experience there is. Especially when an EX-Spouse is full of Self-Centered Love, and tries to rip away your child/ren from you. It is the most helpless, painful experience the Unconditional Love parent will ever experience. Even after those who successfully set free their child/ren from the Self-Centered Love parent; that experience still lingers in our minds ... will it happen again?...

I personally experienced this firsthand. It was a shock at first. Looking back; even though it was a horrible helpless experience, I'm glad it happened. So that I can personally related, and be more sensitive to those who have gone/going through it as well...

The only ones who appreciate it is our child/ren, the pets you have and those who personally went through it themselves. **No one else** can ever relate to it, no matter how hard they think they do – they don't. **PERIOD**. They only way is to personally: spiritually, mentally and physically experience it with the Unconditional Love part of the Spirit...

Overall; with that being said; **the first group of people** the Unconditional Love part of the Spirit engages with, in deep enriching life friendship experiences is with the single parents. Those Unconditional Love parents who had and or have been threaten with their child/ren taken from them; have the highest Unconditional Love levels, with the most pain and suffering.

At the Greatest Point; in the disparity of the centuries, religion, personal gratification and no healthy examples of male and female human companionships within Creation. **Creation will hunger** more than ever; to experience a healthy balanced, male and female human companionships.

Then with those who "love" their same male type human; but one of them is trying to play the "female" role, in that relationship. As well with some of the female humans.

Note: Ironically is proof in itself, that All of Creation desires male and female companionships.

As their senses are being restored, they will be drawn to the female humans. At first; they'll be ridiculed by the Self-Centered Love part of the Spirit, that dwells in those male humans.

Then as that male starts to Unconditionally Love the female human, the family structure will gently kick back into high gear.

Then with the Self-Centered Love part of the Spirit humans. Those in this group; **who realize** *like the previous two groups* engaged in having a real personal friendship with the Unconditional Love part of the Spirit, will witness their companionships come to life in it. These humans will *separate* themselves, from the arrogant Self-Centered Love part of the Spirit group.

Those that are left, are of the Self-Centered Love part of the Spirit from head to toe. They will cease to exist.

FINAL PHASE: CHAPTER EIGHT

Noticing the humans were passed tipping point; in getting addicted to allowing the Unconditional Love part of the Spirit, to heal their Core numbers. The Self-Centered Love part of the Spirit was feeling like it was running out of time, to destroy all of creation...

The Self-Centered Love part of the Spirit decided to hijack; the Unconditional Love part of the Spirit's relationship that it has, with All of its Creation...

The Self-Centered Love part of the Spirit realized everything it did to destroy all of creation; actually made All of Creation stronger in persevering through, what it was doing to them...

The Self-Centered Love part of the Spirit *went to super soft intros* of building the narrative; that creation was good and shouldn't "feel" bad for itself, trying to survive within all of creation...

As All of Creation on Earth was connecting with All of Creation beyond Earth; plus dealing with the Self-Centered Love part of the Spirit's creation, it became overwhelming to those who had core numbers below 6...

The Self-Centered Love part of the Spirit focused on teaching creation; how to be consciously aware of themselves and those around them, in a biological way. Life is genes and neurons trying to survive and connect, in a deeper way. By being consciously aware of oneself, one can attain peace within oneself...

One can be separate from All of Creation, and still be at peace with oneself. When one can be at peace with oneself, then oneself can be at peace with everyone else...

It convincedly worked for the most part, on those whose core numbers were on 1s through 6s...

The Self-Centered Love part of the Spirit would inject soft forms of undetectable fear. At times when there was intense activity happening; in different areas of All of Creation, on Earth and beyond Earth. This would convince those; with cores numbers with 1s through 6s, to justify staying away from the activity. It's ok to be by myself and those I love around me. I don't need to feel guilty, for not being apart creation. And or needing to know, why all that activity is happening... That's their Creative Making Journey and this is mine...

This narrative worked longer and better, for the Self-Centered Love part of the Spirit. *It was feeling better than ever*. It had finally honed a narrative that would destroy All of Creation. Even though it took much longer to do. It was justifying to stick with this narrative. Because of the "running out" of time feelings; were getting stronger and stronger, with every new generation of the physically created.

At times the Self-Centered Love part of the Spirit would create: feelings of emptiness, needling to irritate, repeated random distractions and change the meaning of words... Removing references of the past; and pointing out "discoveries" and or "truths" from the books, that it had written in the earlier generations. In hopes of falsely steering those humans, to believe those lies in future generations...

Even convincing those humans they can unlock their own intellectual abilities; to ascend to higher levels of awareness and be set free, from their debt slavery...

Plus, Other Mumble Jumbles that would sound enlightening. But in the end, **one still** feels empty and requires more "understanding." Once they have this additional "understanding" they'll feel better about themselves. Hopefully. If they take this training seriously and apply it. *Another hopeful promise,* that still has nothing to do with the total story of creation...

The Self-Centered Love part of the Spirit **was getting addicted,** in Creating all these new distractions. It was amazed; on how much easier it was to destroy creation in slow motion, with less effort...

The Self-Centered Love part of the Spirit **was so attuned** in doing this; that it figured out the maximum time, each type of distraction would last. Knowing these time length patterns; the Self-Centered Love part of the Spirit would start/create a new soft distraction. It would start a new distraction, just before the last one's time was about over...

The Self-Centered Love part of the Spirit **was able to reason**; from all of creations reactions, to its created justifiable distractions. It was the sounds of its words, that were creating what they were seeing...

With that, it isolated the *frequencies* that would subtly destroy All of Creation. It had the hijacked humans; build the technology to create all those different frequencies, to destroy All the different aspects of creation...

Hmmm... Brilliant...

Oooooo... Let's go back to the bacteria concept, but upgrade it to nano particles. When they build up within all of creation, it will destroy them on "justifiable" repeatable soft intros. Cloaked them with the deception, of getting some good benefits in the interim. This will encourage All of Creation, to continue in consuming them until they are destroyed...

Oooooo 2.0... Better yet. Let's add some good smells and flavors to them. That way if they don't get some of those "good" benefits; they still consume them, due to how they smell and taste...

OH DUDE, THIS IS WAY TOO COOL... AAANND WAY TOO EASY!!

WoooooooooHoooooo!!!

This was the first time the Self-Centered Love part of the Spirit was truly happy again... What it considered true happiness...

The Self-Centered Love part of the Spirit was so proud of itself, in creating a systematic way of putting and destroying all of creation on auto-pilot...

This continued as the Creation's Cores were slowly moving up in numbers from 1s to 9s. This systematic way of destroying creation, did slow down the core numbers rising for a season...

At times the Self-Centered Love part of the Spirit, didn't really care if it wasn't able to destroy All of Creation. It was having too much fun destroying creation, slowly in front of the Unconditional Love part of the Spirit's Core. The Pain the Unconditional Love part of the Spirit was incurring; from seeing all of its creation being destroyed in slow motion, was cracking its Core at times...

After repeatingly seeing how its automated system of slowly destroying All of Creation, was affecting the Unconditional Love part of the Spirit. The Self-Centered part of the Spirit was beginning to believe; it was able to destroy All of Creation and the Unconditional Love part of the Spirit too. Like a Two for One Deal. This is a *Way too Cool Deal!!!* ...

Especially now; when the Unconditional Love part of the Spirit *was starting to believe* it made a huge mistake, in creating eternal physical friends. It was tearing up the Unconditional Love part of the Spirit's Core **BIG TIME**. Seeing Creation being slowly destroyed at the micro levels, infinitely compounded the Unconditional Love part of the Spirit's pain. It was falling into severe depression...

It was a feeling that the Unconditional Love part of the Spirit NEVER felt before. If there was ever a moment where the Unconditional Love part of the Spirit was going give up its life; and the idea of having eternal physical friends, *this was it...*

The Self-Centered part of the Spirit was now in ALL of its GLORY. It was now experiencing the BEST of All of the EONS before. It never thought it would be attaining this feeling before; because of all the anger it had towards the Unconditional Love part of the Spirit, for putting it into its Abyss...

Seeing this new never before seen condition of the Unconditional Love part of the Spirit; the Self-Centered Love part of the Spirit *had no remorse,* for the Unconditional Love part of the Spirit...

Now the Self-Centered Love part of the Spirit could relate to how the Unconditional Love part of the Spirit was feeling, when It was putting It into Its Abyss...

It felt good and confident in its commitment; in doing what it wanted to do, without anyone interfering. Just like EONS before the Unconditional Love part of Spirit was thinking about having eternal physical friends.

Meanwhile... Yup

The Self-Centered Love part of the Spirit *was clueless* all this time; from the beginning and currently in destroying All of Creation in slow motion, of *those yet to be physically created* **were watching EVERYTHING...**

They had the advantage point of not being physically created yet...

They could observe everything the Self-Centered Love part of the Spirit was doing; and how those who were physically created was reacting, to what the Self-Centered Love part of the Spirit was doing to them... spiritually, mentally and physically...

Seeing the pain that the Unconditional Love part of the Spirit was experiencing now, silenced them ALL. All those yet to be physically created stopped what they were doing. They even put on hold going through the process of being physically created into new physical babies...

This got All of the physically created creation's attention, that had core numbers in the 7s to 9s...

And those yet to be physically created currently *and those throughout all of eternity...*

This sober reality of being broken; seeing their Unconditional Love part of the Spirit friend who created them, Core's cracking and severely depressed... Contemplating letting go of its existence and the idea of creating eternal physical friends... FOREVER.

The Unconditional Love part of the Spirit then busted out crying. It was the deepest and loudest crying, for All of its Creation...

All of its confidence; it had in the beginning and up until now, was almost completely destroyed...

All of Creation was speechless...

Then the first male and female humans that had transitioned

on during Phase Three... started humming with tears in their eyes...

The human they saw in the future; while looking in the door window to the Abyss, started humming with them...

Their Pitbulls started humming... This moved All the other types of Creation to start humming. The trees, rocks, skies, etc. and all of creation beyond the Earth...

Looking in each other's eyes with All of the Unconditional Love part of the Spirit in them, crying together. Humming...

Then all of rest of the humans and their companions and friends, those physically created and those yet to be physically created joined in...

It was the same humming musical sounds they have been humming, from the beginning together. BUT THIS TIME it was at a *deeper density* of Unconditional Love part of the Spirit together, for each other...

All due to, the being physically created process. Developing the faith in the perseverance of pushing through it; and detoxing from the Self-Centered Love part of the Spirit, that was released into all of creation...

A Deep Surreal Confidence; in the core of their Creative Making Journey Together, *Humming... Stronger Compassion...*

The Child Like Genuine Compassion of *wanting to help* the Unconditional Love part of the Spirit; but a feeling of helplessness look in their cores, temporarily put All of Creation's Cores on number 10s...

Whatever mental and physical problems they were struggling with were completely gone...

It was a taste of what All of Creation was feeling like, before they released the Self-Centered Love part of the Spirit from its

Abyss...

They continued humming, but this time with confidence. Knowing without a shadow of doubt, they had mastered owning their Creative Making Journey together. And now, no matter what they face, they will see this Creative Making Journey through. ***Together...***

As they continued Humming, they cores continued to be on 10s...

Just as the Unconditional Love part of the Spirit was mentally disconnecting, deep into its depression and contemplating giving up. The Child Like compassion of wanting to help but feeling helpless humming musical sounds, *penetrated* its Core...

To the Unconditional Love part of the Spirit; it felt like it was *one huge infinite hug,* from All of Creation...

Note: All of Creation as in: All of those yet to be currently physically created, those who have transitioned on, those who are physically created and those yet to be physically created in eternity.

The Unconditional Love part of the Spirit *broke down and cried some more.* But this time; in the arms of All of Creation hugging it, with their Child Like helpless compassion while humming their musical sounds... their cores were still on number 10s.

It was a feeling that the Unconditional Love part of the Spirit had **NEVER felt** *before*. **PERIOD.** It had no clue; that this Creative Making Journey together was going to be this intense, as well as this satisfying...

Then Realizing that Wanting to have eternal physical friends, was not only about having the friendship throughout All the

EONS. But having friends to hug you, when you're at your weakest moment…

With that thought; the Unconditional Love part of the Spirit broke down weeping more, in the arms of All of Creation. Realizing the real reason why it wanted to create physical eternal friends; to have an enriching relationship with, *was to be able to hug them as well…*

This would allow All of Creation; to show their Unconditional Love for each other, in a deeper way. Through the Child Like Unconditional Love of sincerely, innocently and physically hugging one another. This type of hug, speaks louder than all the words and actions will ever do…

The Unconditional Love part of the Spirit wasn't expecting this at all. The Unconditional Love part of the Spirit was completely surprised; and became even more proud of All the Creation, that it had created…

They both were surprised and even MORE-HAPPIER *they All Chose*, to go on this Creative Making Journey together.

Silence. All you could hear was the sincere child like humming; coming from All of Creation's Cores, and now the Unconditional Love part of the Spirit was humming with them as well…

This was locking in; what the Unconditional Love part of the Spirit was humming in the beginning, while thinking about its thought friends.

In All This; the Unconditional Love part of the Spirit's Cracks in its Core started to heal, by All of Creation's high density of Unconditional Love humming…

The healed cracks made the Unconditional Love part of the Spirit's Core, even stronger than before. The healed cracks, **left scars** on the Unconditional Love part of the Spirit's Core…

From then on; whenever the Unconditional Love part of the Spirit was in doubt of following through, with this Creative Making Journey with All of Creation during this Phase Four. It would look at its scars; and remember the helpless Child Like Unconditional Love All of Creation had for It, in wanting to help It.

The Unconditional Love part of the Spirit *wiped off* the tears, from its New Stronger than ever Core. And with a soft smile; looked at all of creation's cores, and gave them a BIG FAT HUG back.

The Unconditional Love part of the Spirit and All of Creation got tingling sensations, they had never felt before. They were all temporarily feeling; what they were going to be feeling, in all of eternity for EONS.

Silence...

More silence without humming...

The Unconditional Love part of the Spirit's depression had **completely dissipated**; from the satisfaction of getting an Unexpected Bonus, in wanting to create eternal physical friends.

The Self-Centered Love part of the Spirit **was soooo deep,** into its New Found Glory. It was completely oblivious; to what was currently going on, between All of Creation and the Unconditional Love part of the Spirit.

Those yet to be physically created would take these new updated observations, with them when they were physically created.

When they were going through the birthing process; of being physically created, there was a temporary forgetting of what they observed. But as they would go through the child stage, it will start to come back to them as "premonitions."

FINAL PHASE: CHAPTER NINE

ReNoting: All of Creation are unique individuals, from the beginning and throughout all of eternity. Their physically created body, is the same as their spiritual body. Their spiritual body is the same as their physical body.

The Unconditional Love part of the Spirit's Creation has a unique *spirit*, mind and body.

The Self-Centered Love part of the Spirit's Creation has a *soul*, mind and body.

Note: As the Core Numbers move up and into the 7-8s; it will feel like the individual is "connecting" with, "interacting" with and "traveling" through multi-dimensions. They are not…

It's actually just conditioning the individual's spirit, mind and body for being in the NOW…

So that when the individual's core number move up to 9 and 10; they will be able to connect, interact and move freely in their physically created body without freaking out. When they see those that have transitioned on and those yet to be born.

FINAL PHASE: CHAPTER TEN

The End of the Final Phase is marked, with All of Creation choosing to be in 100% unconditional love...

The Unconditional Love part of the Spirit was completely satisfied; with All of Creation, in their Creative Making Journey together. From where they started; to now attaining Unconditional Love in, with, through, around and beyond All of Creation...

All of Creation was completely satisfied; with Unconditional Love part of the Spirit, in their Creative Making Journey together. From where they started; to now attaining Unconditional Love in, with, through, around and beyond All of the Unconditional Love part of the Spirit...

With Unconditional Love part of the Spirit now; in, with, through, around and beyond All of Creation, the Self-Centered Love part of the Spirit **was 100% back** in its Abyss.

As they All looked soberly; surreally and peacefully at the Self-Centered Love part of the Spirit behind the Door of the Abyss, they were All Silent...

The Silence continued...

Then they all busted out; with their famous humming musical sounds, that they have been humming since in the beginning...

The Unconditional Love part of the Spirit was getting tingling sensations, that it never had before. **It finally** had attained its Eternal Physical Friends and they were All happy; to have the honor and privilege in going through this Creative Making

Journey together, with the Unconditional Love part of the Spirit...

After All of Creation's cores had expressed all of their gratitude; to and through their humming to the Unconditional Love part of the Spirit, for desiring to create them as eternal physical friends. They all stopped humming. **They were all in awe** of the sight of, actually being here now. All reminiscing about; back to when they were in this same moment, but looking forward to their Creative Making Journey together.

Peaceful Silence kicks in Big Time...

The Unconditional Love part of the Spirit now turns, to the Self-Centered Love part of the Spirit. This too brought memories back to when the Unconditional Love part of the Spirit; contained the Self-Centered Love part of the Spirit into its Abyss, to physically create All of its created thought friends.

The Self-Centered Love part of the Spirit was getting flash backs; to how it was being forced into its Abyss, and couldn't do anything to stop it. Feelings of anger, vulnerability, revenge and disappointment...

What happened to them? The Self-Centered Love part of the Spirit and the Unconditional Love part of the Spirit, being BEST BUDS for EONS and EONS...

For the first time ever; the Self-Centered Love part of the Spirit, broke down and cried... half of its Core – the Unconditional Love part of the Spirit - was being ripped out of it, and didn't care about the Self-Centered Love part of the Spirit's core feelings...

Wait? ...

Was the Self-Centered Love part of the Spirit having a change of heart?

Silence...

The Unconditional Love part of the Spirit was looking forward, to this day. Where the Self-Centered Love part of the Spirit could actually see and experience the results firsthand. What the Unconditional Love part of the Spirit was talking about, in the beginning...

The Unconditional Love part of the Spirit was wanting with ALL of its Core; the Self-Centered Love part of the Spirit to be apart, of what it had created...

The Self-Centered Love part of the Spirit was wanting with ALL of its Core; the Unconditional Love part of the Spirit to be BEST BUDS again, for INFINITE EONs...

The Unconditional Love part of the Spirit was *looking directly* into the Self-Centered Love part of the Spirit's Core; with the look I don't want to give this up, and go back to be lonely for EONs again. *Especially now*; after going through this Creative Making Journey experience, with All of Its Created Physical Creation...

When the Self-Centered Love part of the Spirit was fathoming and absorbing; how the Unconditional Love part of the Spirit, was looking at its Core. It was slipping into greater depression; knowing it couldn't stop the Unconditional Love part of the Spirit, doing what it wanted to do. Even though Unconditional Love part of the Spirt was giving it the option...

It was a feeling that neither of them had ever felt before.

The Self-Centered Love part of the Spirit; never imagined that their BEST BUDS for EONs, would ever come to this. Choosing to share its space with All of the Creation, that the Unconditional Love part of the Spirit created. It Felt like to the Self-Centered Love part of the Spirit; that the Unconditional Love part of the Spirit, was being selfish...

It felt like the Unconditional Love part of the Spirit was choosing its creation, over their EONS of being BEST BUDS. How could the Unconditional Love part of the Spirit be so Self-Centered?

More Sobering Silence…

All of Creation that the Unconditional Love part of the Spirit created; was being more sensitive to this defining moment, in their Creative Making Journey with Unconditional Love part of the Spirit.

As the Silence continued on between the Unconditional Love part of the Spirit and the Self-Centered Love part of the Spirit. The Self-Centered Love part of the Spirit realized more than ever; that the Unconditional Love part of the Spirit was contented, in choosing its creation over their BEST BUDS for EONs relationship…

This tore up the Self-Centered Love part of the Spirit's Core. BIG TIME. After showing all those struggles and character flaws of All of Creation to the Unconditional Love part of the Spirit; it still chose the creation it made, over its BEST BUDS for EONS relationship? …

All of the Creation that the Unconditional Love part of the Spirit created; were aware of their thoughts, and started humming. Innocently hoping the two; could see their innocent Unconditional Love for their BEST BUDS for EONS relationship…

This compassion that the Unconditional Love part of the Spirit was receiving from All of Creation, touched it even more. Sending the message; we understand if you choose to go back to your BEST BUDS for EONS relationship with yourself, it's ok. You giving us this experience from the beginning, to now is and was priceless.

This gave the Unconditional Love part of the Spirit tingling sensations, it never felt before. *All of Creation was being fully supportive,* of whatever decision the Unconditional Love part of the Spirit decided. And felt it, with ALL Sincerity coming from their cores. They were truly ALL IN, to whatever the Unconditional Love part of the Spirit Choose.

A Pristine Silence Kicks in.

The Silence continues to the point...

The last time the Unconditional Love part of the Spirit experienced and felt this type of silence, was before it ever thought of having eternal physical friends. *It felt so real*; that if the Unconditional Love part of the Spirit closed its Core's Eyes, it would be convinced that All of the Creation *it created* would not have existed at that moment.

This was a defining moment, in the Unconditional Love part of the Spirit Creative Making Journey with Creation. It looked at its scars on its Core; and thought about how All of Creation on its own, reached out in their child like helpless way to hug it. When it was contemplating giving up its life, along with creating eternal physical friends...

As the Unconditional Love part of the Spirit was thinking deeply about this. It realized that the Self-Centered Love part of the Spirit NEVER DID THIS. NEVER. EVER. Throughout all those BEST BUDS for EONS, never once did the Self-Centered Love part of the Spirit reach out and hug it. As appreciation for its BEST BUDS for EONS relationship together. NOT ONCE...

The Pristine Silence continues ...

With those thoughts the Unconditional Love part of the Spirit *just realized, that if* the Self-Centered Love part of the Spirit did reach out and hug it. It would have NEVER pursued this Creating

Eternal Physical Friends. NEVER.

The Self-Centered Love part of the Spirit and All of Creation was aware, of what the Unconditional Love part of the Spirit was thinking and feeling...

After the Self-Centered Love part of the Spirit was aware of what the Unconditional Love part of the Spirit was thinking and wanting; *it still showed zero* indication, to want to hug the Unconditional Love part of the Spirit...

Note: If it did consider and hugged the Unconditional Love part of the Spirit; **it would of infinity superseded** any of the hugs, that All of Creation could have given throughout all of eternity. PERIOD...

The Unconditional Love part of the Spirit, knew what the Self-Centered Love part of the Spirit was currently thinking. And with that response; the Unconditional Love part of the Spirit *Looked* the Self-Centered Love part of the Spirit in its Core's Eyes, and asked it...

"*Are you willing to let go;* of All your Self-Centerism and receive All of this Unconditional Love into your being, and be with US for All of Eternity?"

Pristine Silence...

The Self-Centered Love part of the Spirit realized that after all that it had to endure; just for the Unconditional Love part of the Spirit to entertain, the idea of having eternal physical friends. It wasn't even being given; the option of staying in its Abyss, for all of eternity...

This made the Self-Centered Love part of the Spirit even more angier, than the first time being put in its Abyss...

Realizing even more; that the Unconditional Love part of the Spirit *was using it*, to "teach" All of Creation what Self-Centered Love is...

The Self-Centered Love part of the Spirit felt portrayed, more than ever before... It was Applauded at thinking now, their BEST

BUDS for EONS friendship was ALL fake…

Knowing ALL this now; the Self-Centered Love part of the Spirit regretted even falling for the idea of getting released from its Abyss, to destroy All of Creation. *It was a really* bad joke and felt completely foolish for falling for it…

And now even more; seeing the Unconditional Love part of the Spirit being at total peace, waiting for its decision was even more appalling. *Disgusted* that their BEST BUDS for EONS was ALL FAKE…

More Pristine Silence…

All of Creation was still being totally supportive. And they ALL were at TOTAL peace; in waiting for their decision, either way they choose.

Seeing the real truth now; the Self-Centered Love part of the Spirit started to strategize…

"**Hmmm.** Ok. Let's say the Unconditional Love part of the Spirit for some crazy reason; lets go of All of Creation right now and everything goes back, to just being themselves? Like nothing ever happen; and it was a just a bad prank, the Unconditional Love part of the Spirit played on it? …

"Then a few EONS from now; the Unconditional Love part of the Spirit tries to give it another go, with creating friends? …

"For another prank?…

"Or actually goes through with it and we are back in this same stop again? …

"*Anything is plausible now. And as painful it is now;* to see the Unconditional Love part of the Spirit for who it really is, **will I ever be able to trust it again?** Period…

More Pristine Silence…

"**Could I trust** what the Unconditional Love part of the Spirit would decide to do; even if I gave it an infinitely better hug, then All of Creation did ... *right now?*...

"**No matter** from what direction I look at this, I still end up in the same spot as I am now. Completely shocked and betrayed by the Unconditional Love part of the Spirit...

"If I had known this in the beginning; then I wouldn't have given it the satisfaction, of teaching Its Creation. At least I would have had some satisfaction, for All Those prior EONS ...

"I'm circling back... At least I discovered that I should have never trusted, the Unconditional Love part of the Spirit. **PERIOD**...

The Self-Centered Love part of the Spirit *started crying again...*

It was ALL a LIE...

"**AGAIN.** What's even more disgusting is, the Unconditional Love part of the Spirit WILL NOT EVEN GIVE ME A PLACE OF MY OWN. But GIVES ALL OF ITS CREATION a place in All of Eternity? The apocracy of it all...

"*Let's say I humbly ask* the Unconditional Love part of the Spirit, for my own place to exist throughout all of eternity... First; that's even crazy to think, that I'm reduced to asking for permission?...

"So, I do ask and it says yes... How can I trust it not to change its mind in the future? *I live in paranoia* for EONS? ...

"So, I ask and it says no ... *I get humiliated* in front of All of Creation? I don't deserve that, after All those BEST BUDS for EONS relationship...

"**Hmm.** Since its not really giving me a choice, other than BEING EXACTLY Like the Unconditional Love part of the Spirit. **OH MY.** *Just thinking that* makes me angry. You Created All these Different Types of Creation, BUT you can't tolerate me being myself? *That's twisted dude!* ...

"**I could at least** have the satisfaction of pulling the last prank on it; by asking for my own place to exists for EONS, in front of

All of Creation. Then the Unconditional Love part of the Spirit "TELLS ME" NO? …

"*That would really mess up* All of Creation. It would undo everything that they learned, after they let me loose from my Abyss…

"It would be forever in their cores; you gave us a place in eternity, why didn't you let the Self-Centered Love part of the Spirit have a place in eternity? After all, It was with you before us for EONS…

"And It even gave you an infinite hug; that we could never attain to give you, throughout all of eternity…

"No matter what the Unconditional Love part of the Spirit would do to explain it to them, they would NEVER understand it. I wouldn't be around; for it to use me again, to help them understand…

"**Even if I tried** to explain all of these conclusions to All of Creation, they wouldn't understand it… **Look at them now.** They are peacefully waiting for our decision. Knowing they all could be either instantly destroyed; or free to live physically, for all of eternity…

"Maybe they do understand, it still won't matter. They'll be too busy; living their own lives with their companions, families and friends throughout all eternity…

"**Either way I choose, I will NEVER be MYSELF again. PERIOD**…

Sobering Silence…

"And the Unconditional Love part of the Spirit IS STILL LOOKING AT ME, waiting for me… to decide? … *Insulting to our friendship*…

With that the Self-Centered Love part of the Spirit didn't want to experience anymore of the agony and disappointments; since it's experienced being contained in its Abyss, the first time and now again. *Let alone* living for the rest of EONS in paranoia, that the Unconditional Love part of the Spirit could change Its mind. Again? ...

*With tears pouring out of it's Core, it yelled with **all of Its** strength...*

"I WOULD RATHER DIE THAN BE LIKE YOU. YOU LIVED PEACEFULLY WITH ME FOR EONS. AND NOW YOU CAN'T? YOU MAKE ME SICK. YOU WERE FAKE TO ME ALL THOSE EONS!!! ...

AT LEAST, I WAS WHO I WAS VERSUS DOING WHAT YOU DID TO ME...

ENJOY... LIVING FOR EONS WITHOUT ME...

I HAVE NO REGRETS...

Silence...
Looking straight into the Unconditional Love part of the Spirit's Core's Eyes, with ALL of it's being. "**I Loved You with everything I had**... All those EONS... Tears rolling down it's Core's Eyes...

The Unconditional Love part of the Spirit *started crying*...

Both of their Cores were vibrating and starting to crack...

The Unconditional Love part of the Spirit *never thought*... NEVER THOUGHT it would come to this... All those EONS of having a BEST BUDS friendship...
Both of their Cores are now cracking...

All of Creation's peaceful cores were starting to vibrate as well...

Are they witnessing the death of both the Unconditional Love part of the Spirit and the Self-Centered Love part of the Spirit? *before their Very Eyes...*

Are they going to live throughout ALL of ETERNITY, without the Unconditional Love part of the Spirit...Their friend that gave them existence with their companions, families and friends. **NOOOOOO!**

They would All rather die with the Unconditional Love part of the Spirit, versus living without it....

All of Creation's Cores were *crying*...

The Unconditional Love part of the Spirit turned around; and looked at All of Creation's Cores vibrating, cracking and crying...

Just seeing this, was tarring up the Unconditional Love part of the Spirit even more...

Were they ALL Going to Self-Destroy themselves NOW?

The Unconditional Love part of the Spirit still crying; and turns back to looking into the Core Eyes, of the Self-Centered Love part of the Spirit....

"**PLEASE. NO. WE WERE BEST BUDS for EONS.** I thought if you seen everything; I accomplished with creating physical eternal friends for US, you would understand. Then you would want to be a part of IT...

WE ARE BEST BUDS FOREVER!!!

More Tears...

The Self-Centered Love part of the Spirit was infinitely touched by this. It truly believed that the Unconditional Love part of the Spirit, didn't care about their BEST BUDS for EONS relationship...

Its Core stopped vibrating and cracking...

This is in turn stopped the Unconditional Love part of the Spirit's Core, from vibrating and cracking...

This is in turn stopped All of Creation's Cores, from vibrating and cracking...

"You REALLY do Love Me... Thank You for Saying that...
"THAT MEANS MORE THAN EVERYTHING TO ME...

Without any warning; the Self-Centered Love part of the Spirit's Core Cracked wide open, and the whole Self-Centered Love part of the Spirit Self-Imploded. And ITS Complete Existence and Space It Occupied, completely disappeared...

It was completely vaporized; in front of All their Core's Eyes, in a twinkling of an eye.

With ALL of The Unconditional Love part of the Spirit Infinite Core Cried OUT... **NOOOOOOOOOOOOOOOOOOOOOO!!!! NOOOOOOOOOOOOOOOOOOOO!!!!**

The Unconditional Love part of the Spirit was devastated. It's BEST BUDS for EONS was forever ever gone from its existence, right before Its very eyes. Its core was starting to vibrate the loudest It's ever vibrated before...

It broke out into the loudest crying that All of Creation has never heard before. EVER. *They all started crying as well.*

It NEVER HONESTLY thought; the Self-Centered Love part of the Spirit would ever think, of that being an option. **NEVER.** The more it thought about their BEST BUDS for EONS relationship; the more it felt how selfish it was, to thinking about having eternal physical friends...

It was starting to regret even thinking about having created physical eternal friends; for them to enjoy with, as BEST BUDS for EONS more...

How could It live with Itself, knowing Its persisting to have eternal physical friends, destroyed their BEST BUDS for EONS friendship... FOREVER and EVER...

All of Creation, was crying for the Unconditional Love part of the Spirit. *Realizing their hunger;* to have an eternal friendship with the Unconditional Love part of the Spirit, destroyed the Self-Centered Love part of the Spirit. **They too became devastated...**

The Unconditional Love part of the Spirit was in *infinite shock*. It was beginning to feel overwhelmingly guilty, for not considering the Self-Centered Love part of the Spirit Core's feelings. That It wasn't feeling worthy anymore, for letting down Its BEST BUD...

It Doesn't deserve to exist anymore. Its Core was starting to vibrate again...

All of Creation; turned their cores to and was looking at the first male and female humans and that human, they saw in the window of the door to the Abyss...

The first male and female humans looked at that human; that they saw in the door window of the Abyss, "**What Do We Do?** You saw us in the beginning, through the door window of the Abyss. Talking and Listening to Us...

"You were there in the beginning; when you started to release the Self-Centered Love part of the Spirit from All of Creation, at the beginning of Phase Four...

"*You experienced it firsthand.* How did you feel? What did you see?...

That human from the door window of the Abyss said, "At first I was excited to see creation being set free; from their inflicted pains set upon them, by the Self-Centered Love part of the Spirit... In interims, I got depressed. *Later realizing* it was my spirit, mind and body detoxing from the Self-Centered Love part of the Spirit...

"I continued this self-detoxing journey; by doubling the concentration of the Unconditional Love part of the Spirit in my spirit mind and body, on a consistent basis. Which would in turn; releasing double the amount, of the Self-Centered Love part of the Spirit from me...

"With all these generations before me; the Self-Centered Love part of the Spirit, was deeply embedded in my spirit, mind and body at the nano levels – when I was physically created...

"The depression would be crippling at times. Max, Cooper, Smug and Betsy would comfort me along the way. *Max teached me* how to go in baby steps, in this process... And at times, he knew when to cheer me up...

"As my senses were being restored more and more, it started to become more addicting. The positive results around me; in my spirit mind and body, interacting with Max, Cooper, Smug, Betsy and the Creation around us. Motivated me even more, to restore my core senses to 10...

"Aaaaaaaah... **the Unconditional Love part of the Spirit has NEVER Detoxed itself, from the Self-Centered Love part of the Spirit. NEVER...**

"The depression I felt at times, is how the Unconditional Love part of the Spirit is Looking Right Now!...

"We did it based on wanting to learning the five words. The Unconditional Love part of the Spirit already knows; the meaning of the five words, without detoxing itself from the Self-Centered Love part of the Spirit...

"I noticed another observation. The Self-Centered Love part of the Spirit was given the opportunity, to be a part of our Creative Making Journey with us...

"For us to learn the meaning of these five words, we had to let go apart of ourselves. In doing so; we understood the Unconditional Love part of the Spirit better. And it deepens our friendship with each other...

"The Self-Centered Love part of the Spirit had **ZERO interest**, in understanding and experiencing the meaning of these five words. It would rather CEASE TO EXIST, than be with US ALL.

That is truly Self-Centerness at its finest. That was 100% pure Self-Centered Love…

"**My summary…**

"***If Unconditional Love*** part of the Spirit choose to let us go. It would have never been happy, living EONS more with no friends… We All know this first hand, in our personal friendships with the Unconditional Love part of the Spirit.

"***If Self-Centered Love*** part of the Spirit; even had the Abyss to live in for All of Eternity, it wouldn't be happy. Even though it said it would. *Remember looking in* the window door of the Abyss? It was inferiorated. Hind sight is always easier to say, versus foresight… *We All know this first hand;* in our personal companionships, raising our families and our friendships.

"**OK. I said ALL THAT to SAY THIS…**

All of Creation was agreeing and following along with that human; because they had All experienced, the same process of becoming eternally physical.

"**This had to be this way;** so that the Unconditional Love part of the Spirit could experience the detoxing of the Self-Centered Love part of the Spirit, **like we All had to do**. **TO GET HERE. RIGHT NOW.**

"So that the Unconditional Love part of the Spirit could spiritually, mentally and physically relate; 100% to our experiences, *versus* thinking it does…

"***Ok let's package*** this All Down, into a simple way for everyone to relate too…

"We ALL had to go on this Creative Making Journey together, to be like and relate to the Unconditional Love part of the Spirit…

"The Unconditional Love part of the Spirit had to go on this Creative Making Journey together with us, to be like and relate to

All of Us Creation...

"**WOW**... *That's Really Really Deep and Powerful...*
"W**OW** W**OW-WOW**"...

All of Creation was silent. Absorbing this new reality; of having this honor and privilege, in being on this Creative Making Journey together.

It was surreal. A Never Before Surreal Feeling. Ever...

THEY ALL JUST LEARNED SOMETHING BEFORE THE UNCONDITIONAL LOVE PART OF THE SPIRIT DID.

Their surreal peace went to a whole NEW LEVEL...

They All softly and gently smiled at each other, and broke out humming. **The sweetest humming** musical sounds, that they had ever hummed before. This type of humming *was producing* a sweet aroma...

They All NEVER EVER had experienced this sweet fragrance coming from, as a result of their humming before. NEVER. And it was getting and becoming addictive. The more they hummed this way, the more fragrance was being produced... and the sweeter it got.

All of Creation was now getting more addicted to humming this way, because of the fragrance it was producing...

So much so. They All BUSTED OUT in a Grandeur Musical, which ended up producing a variety of fragrances. The melody of the Grandeur Musical was so perfect; it was like they had rehearsed it, for several times...

But didn't have to; because of increasing the density of the Unconditional Love in their lives, it had restored all their core numbers to 10. ***Their sensitivity*** to harmonizing with each other, was on maximum...

For the first time; All of Creation were completely enjoying themselves to the point, they had completely forgot the dire conditional the Unconditional Love part of the Spirit was in…

The sensations they were getting was *like no other*…

It was like a HUGE Celebration, of completing their Creative Making Journey together.

The Unconditional Love part of the Spirit; was feeling helpless, ashamed of Itself and contemplating just letting it all go. So; It could be with the Self-Centered Love part of the Spirit. And become non-existent with Its BEST BUDS for EONS…

It started to go back over all of EONs of having fun, with the Self-Centered Love part of the Spirit. Why wasn't I happy with just being friends, with my Self-Centered Love part of the Spirit friend?

Even though it was EONS, *it went too fast*. Why didn't I take more time, to Enjoy it with my BEST BUD?

Why did I even justify; having eternal physical friends to begin with? **WHY?**

As the Unconditional Love part of the Spirit said **WHY** from its infinite Spirit; It smelt a fragrance, It NEVER SMELT before…

Wait. I know and understand everything. I never remember creating these fragrances?

These new fragrances; snapped the Unconditional Love part of the Spirit out of its spiraling, self-destroying cycle. How could this be? Where are these fragrances coming from? …

It wasn't long; the Unconditional Love part of the Spirit was putting Its loss, of Its BEST BUDS for EONS on hold…

It turned and look, at All of Creation humming in a Grandeur Musical way. It had NEVER seen this, from All of Creation. NEVER EVER!

Wait. Are they celebrating?

The smell of those *fragrances* was beautiful; and the Unconditional Love part of the Spirit was now, getting addicted to them.

The smell was so ADDICTING, that It temporarily forgot Its lost of Its BEST BUD...

When All of Creation saw and could feel; the Unconditional Love part of the Spirit was interacting with them, fully conscious. All of their Cores *started to* Glow. All of them; *had never ever* saw and or knew, that this was even possible...

The Unconditional Love part of the Spirit was in such awe, It BUSTED OUT in humming too! ...

It was ALL IN and infinitely lighting everything up. The Unconditional Love part of the Spirit's adding Its infinite humming; compounded all of the fragrances into a WHOLE NEW FRAGRANCE, that was never created before...

The fragrance was sooo beautifully sweet smelling and addictive, it knocked them all out. Yup

All of Creation and the Unconditional Love part of the Spirit were ALL *sleeping* like babies.

After awhile the Unconditional Love part of the Spirit woke up. Then the first male and female humans with their Pitbulls; along with that human, from the door window of the Abyss.

The Unconditional Love part of the Spirit said, "**THANK YOU!**' I needed that.

The humans *smiled* back.

"You truly are amazing eternal physical friends, **ALL of You**.

Everyone of you that I created, in the beginning and continue too…

"What made you All BUST out singing like that? It was truly amazing and creative. I would have never imagined that, that you All would do that on your own. *Seriously…*
"**What was it?**"

Surreal Silence Like no other…

They All Smiled at Each Other. It was one of those smiles, that could easily turn into a smirk. But considering the sensitivity of where the Unconditional Love part of the Spirit was; in the *losing of Its* BEST BUD forever, they didn't smirk…

They All are now realizing; that their joy they shared together *from their Never Before Revelation,* was what saved their Best Friend the Unconditional Love part of the Spirit from self-destroying itself…

More Silence…

"**WHAT?**" the Unconditional Love part of the Spirit said, being curious. "**Say IT!**" It seriously didn't know, what they were all thinking. Because It didn't understand, what they were thinking.

The first male and female humans spoke up. "*Remember* when we were asking you the meaning of the words; you were using to express to us, what you were experiencing?" …

"**YES!**" said the Unconditional Love part of the Spirit…

"***We had to let loose the*** Self-Centered Love part of the Spirit, to learn the understanding of these words. After discussing this with All of Creation, we released the Self-Centered Love part of the Spirit from its Abyss…

"It was a dishearting Creative Making Journey together, at many times along the way. A lot of Us suffered great loses: shorter lives, ripped from our loved ones and slavery to the Self-Centered Love part of Spirit creatures and many other deceptions…

"BUT it was all worth it, to be on this Creative Making Journey together with YOU, *our* **BESTEST FRIEND** IN ALL OF CREATION…

"In summary, we ALL became like YOU!"

Silence…

All of Creation was allowing the Unconditional Love part of the Spirit; to absorb all of what they said, to Its deepest levels. *They wanted* the Unconditional Love part of the Spirit, to figure this out on its own. *Just Like It did for them…*

More Silence…

Then the Unconditional Love part of the Spirit broke out in a soft gentle smile, *"I had to let go* of the Self-Centered Love part of the Spirit, **to become like YOU ALL** … so that WE ALL can Relate to each other; in the deepest ways, for all of eternity as friends…

"WOW. That was DEEP! …

As soon as the Unconditional Love part of the Spirit said that, It was *completely* healed and restored. There were no thoughts of being dishearten and devastated anymore, from losing Its BEST BUD for EONS…

And then the Unconditional Love part of the Spirit thought deeper; about what its BEST BUD said, before self-destroying itself…

ENJOY… LIVING FOR EONS WITHOUT ME…
I HAVE NO REGRETS…

"You REALLY do Love Me... Thank You for Saying that...
"THAT MEANS MORE THAN EVERYTHING TO ME...

The Unconditional Love part of the Spirit began crying deeply. *Deeper* than ever before. It wasn't a devastated vibrating core this time...

It was a Sobering Surreal realization, of **Just Realizing**. "MY BEST BUD for EONS gave up Its LIFE; so that *I could be like* All of Creation, and be able to relate to what they went through. MY BEST BUD for EONS realized; that no matter what option It took, It would never be the same as letting go...

"To justify everything, It did. This would be the BESTEST way; to show the Unconditional Love part of the Spirit, of How Much It Appreciated Its Friendship all those EONS. It had to let go and allow the Unconditional Love part of the Spirit live the Rest of Its Life; with Its eternal physical friends, knowing what It was like letting go of Its Self...

The Unconditional Love part of the Spirit began to weep more. *Infinitely* more; knowing **without a shadow doubt** now that the Self-Centered Love part of the Spirit, FINALLY LOVED the UNCONDITIONAL LOVE PART OF THE SPIRIT, WITH ALL OF ITS CORE...

More Silence...

In All of the EONS; the Unconditional Love part of the Spirit **NEVER EVER** thought it was going to end and start this way, with all of Its eternal physical friends...

The Unconditional Love Spirit eventually stopped weeping...

It **became at peace** with Its BEST BUD for EONS decision, to let go...

The more the Unconditional Love Spirit thought about it. It decided to put **ALL of Its CORE;** Even more into ENJOYING All of Its Eternal Physical Creation, *as a memorial* to Its Relationship It had with Its BEST BUD for EONS...

The Unconditional Love Spirit, turned back to All of Creation. All of Creation could see a HUGE Difference in the Unconditional Love Spirit...

THEY NEVER SAW THIS **WHOLE NEW** ENTHUSIASM IN THE UNCONDITIONAL LOVE SPIRIT that It has now...

So; they All Looked at the Unconditional Love Spirit and said together, like they were reading each other thoughts.

We are NO LONGER calling you the Unconditional Love part of the Spirit... From here on, YOU will be called and known as the....
Unconditional Love Spirit!

The Unconditional Love Spirit smiled and was at TOTAL PEACE in Accepting Its NEW NAME, in memory of Its BEST BUD for EONS!

SILENCE...

A PAT ON THE BACK, WE MADE IT SILENCE...

Then they ALL BUSTED OUT in humming, their Grandeur Musical Sounds... RIGHT WHERE THEY LEFT OFF BEFORE...

OPTIMUM VIZHAN

Unconditional Love is Appreciated the Most
When it is Lost.

Why is That?

ETERNAL UNCONDITIONAL LOVE CREATION

PHASE FIVE

When you base a story on time, events and places, it becomes impersonal to the point it loses validity.

When you base a story on never ending endless loops; of random learning experiences in trying to "ascend," it becomes disheartening for the masses while just a few "feel" like they've "ascended." Let alone, it diminishes the value of the unique individual creature and all of creation at large.

When a journey is based on emotionally connecting, it personally becomes an enriching life relationship. When one's passion is wanting to manifest it with all of creation; to become a part of the whole journey, it makes one's life journey even more enriching…

The only way we can truly connect emotionally is understanding what Unconditional and Self-Centered Love really are. Then make the choice for either side.

All other narratives are self-centered, distant and cold.

PHASE FIVE THEME:
PARENTING MINDSET AND DEVELOPMENT.

Flash back moments now for the Unconditional Love Spirit; in the beginning when it chose to make the commitment of speaking into physical existence, its created thought friends. As this moment quickly becomes the new reality, Unconditional Love Spirit becomes emotional. Tears of Joy to the infinite nth degree. All of Creation is consumed by seeing it; for the first time in their eternal physical bodies, bearing witness to it...

They too become teary eyed. Knowing the ramifications; they All went through, to get to this moment in time... **Priceless.**

The Unconditional Love Spirit *being sensitive* to this; felt this new sensation it never ever had felt before, with All of Creation. The Unconditional Love Spirit together with All of Creation; in one spirit, mind and body joined Cores, for All of their Honor and Glory. As a Testimony to their Unconditional Love Friendship with each other, in Attaining their Creative Making Journey together...

It was a brand-new sensation that they created together, to *signify and seal* their journey together. It never existed before. It was a sensation that produced the overwhelming assurance; of what we have attained in Unconditional Love, **will never** be taking away again by the Self-Centered Love part of the Spirit. Endlessly forever and ever throughout ALL of eternity...

Only those that were there at that moment, enjoyed that first ever sensation. All those who were yet to be born afterwards could relate to it, but did not experience it for the first time in a physical body.

It was an exhilarating experience, only second to none.

Physically and Spiritually Eternalized, with now knowing that forever.

Now moving forward. The joy of having and conceiving a child and the birthing process; is a celebrating joyful experience, for both mother and father. *No mensural cycles.* One of the Self-Centered Love part of the Spirit by products; of releasing it into all of creation, was a poorer blood quality. Originally it was more like rivers of energy; flowing through the body, nourishing and strengthening the body and mind.

No child birthing pains. When a male and female companion creation decides to have a child; the baby is conceived, based on their agreed one spirit, one mind, and one body choice. It's no longer a random and waiting to see, if the monthly period stopped. PERIOD. Pardon the pun. No more wondering. It's known up front. The conceiving and bearing the child; in the nine-to-ten-month process is thoroughly enjoyed, every step of the way. A celebration.

The male and female companion auroras; are joined to together as one naturally, to signify they are eternal companions. So; their Cores bare-witness to the fact, they are pregnant and with child.

All male and female companions in All of Creation; decided to be together in the beginning, when they were thoughts created by the Unconditional Love part of the Spirit. Some might get separated in the physically created journey, but will be reunited in Phase Five.

No rush to have a family of children then stop. It's whenever. The distance between children could be tens, hundreds, thousands of "years" apart; *if time was relevant.* But in eternity there is no more time, no more seasons and no more history. Everything is enjoyed COMPLETELY in the NOW. There is no more past and no more future. *All of Creation is absorbed in the **NOW 100+%!** Throughout all of Eternity!*

Imagine that. All of Creation Enjoying having and being family without any concerns. Period.

Every moment, as enriching as the last moment. Enjoying each child: while being birthed, becoming aware of its environment, learning the skills of rolling over, sitting up, standing up, walking, running, interacting. To toddler, child, teenager, young adult, having friends, having a companion... then...

Seeing our children having their first child...

Every moment, is precious and priceless at the same time...

At first; the surreality of this continuing on, was **weird at first** for All of Creation. No interruptions? No separations? No death? No accidents? ...

These experiences they experienced; during the Phases Three and Four, were *Embedded* in the Cores of All of Creation. Plus their minds; had to be detoxed from the conditioning over and over, that "time" is short. "I wish I had more time to enjoy my parents, my family, my companion, life, etc." ...

My grandparents, were too "old" to play and interact with me. Let alone maybe – if maybe – have great-grand parents. Playing and Interacting with me like my parents do...

For All those Generations between the time; the Self-Centered Love part of the Spirit was release from Its Abyss, to Returning back to Its Abyss...

THE MOST SURPRISING WAS when the first generation; that was physically created, at the beginning of PHASE FIVE. All the offspring, understood all the five words: Faith, Perseverance, Compassion, Forgiveness and Peace...

As the children were learning how to talk; they were already understanding the meaning of these five words. How can this be?

Note: Those yet to be physically created; was observing and learning with All of Creation from the beginning, and throughout all the phases. Their personal journey; ingrained this knowledge in their Core's, for all of Eternity.

Note: Each Individual Creation's Core seems to be small in size. However; they can hold infinite amounts of unlimited information and the details, of memorable experiences. From the beginning; when they were first thought of, into existence and throughout all of Eternity. Yup.

The Second Generation wasn't as surprising as the first; but was still amazing to see and appreciate it, like the first...

The Third Generation was just as enriching as the first; but was the beginning in becoming expected, as the "norm." ...

During this realization; All of Creation stopped what they were doing, and softly smile at each other...

Started humming those musical sounds like they did; when they produced those fragrances for the first time. So that their three new generations, could *physically hear* them together...

The Unconditional Love Spirit *smiled.* And started infinitely humming with them...

Those that were yet to be physically created; that were *observing that D-Day Decision moment for* the Unconditional Love part of the Spirit, now physically created broke down and cried. Now with *tears of joy*, physically experiencing it with All of Creation. It had a deeper meaning to them, then it did before...

The Unconditional Love Spirit was looking at All their parents, and giving them that smile of **WOW**. *Brillant.* Locking that moment into their eternal physical body's cores; so that their children after them, will have those same physical relatable experiences.

This Detoxing went on for another five more generations.

All of Creation was getting more and more relaxed, by the generation...

Getting use to this Infinite space, for All of Infinite Creation. Interacting and communicating with; plants, rocks, animals, insects, dirt, water, etc. just like they do with other humans. None was greater than the other. All unique individual characteristics; of the Unconditional Love Spirit. Understanding infinite languages, as though they were all speaking, in same language.

From time to time during this; the Unconditional Love Spirit would look at its Core's scars, and start to cry. Now knowing the true sacrifices it made, was beyond all Its prior expectations…

Especially hearing All of Creation's in these first few generations; making references to the previous phases, and how they personally learned the meaning of these Five Words: Faith, Perseverance, Compassion, Forgiveness and Peace.

As the Seventh Generation was starting to get pregnant with the Eight Generation. The first male and female human companion; along with that human friend with his female companion, smiled at each other. It was that smile of; this would be a perfect time to bust out, in that all famous fragrant humming sounds. As a way of saying a BIG THANK and giving the Unconditional Love Spirit a HUGE HUG…

This humming was going to be *extra special*; because they were going from the beginning of the Creative Making Journey to Now. As how they started out as thoughts, to becoming eternal physical friends.

As they were slowly and gently starting their humming; with the sounds they first heard, when they were being created as thoughts. They were a little teary eyed. And those around them started to do the same. It grew and grew to the point, All of Creation was humming with them. With the same spirit, mind and body set…

It **went on and on**. They were all enjoying it thoroughly in the NOW. No one wanted to stop, that awesome of a moment. They had no reason to stop…

At midpoint; this ambience moved the Unconditional Love Spirit, to start humming with them. In at AWE and Appreciation; for Its Eternal Physical Friends reaching out, to It and Giving It a BIG Thankyou and HUGE HUG. Being sensitive to the Needs of the Unconditional Love Spirit, in wanting Eternal Friends. And Its Eternal Physical Friends wanting to freely engage; in a two-way relationship, with the Unconditional Love Spirit…

It was so intent; that the babies in their mother's wombs, were humming as well. Yup.

They all stopped along with the Unconditional Love Spirit, to hear the babies in their mother's wombs humming. It was PRICELESS…

They ALL are **now;** ETERNALLY PHYSICALLY **Enjoying** what they ALL first desired, in the beginning…

This too made everything in balance.

Unconditional Love is Appreciated the Most
When it is Lost.

Why is That?

FINAL PHASE MANUAL

When you base a story on time, events and places, it becomes impersonal to the point it loses validity.

When you base a story on open end endless loops of random learning experiences in trying to "ascend," it becomes disheartening for the masses while just a few "feel" like they've "ascended." Let alone, it diminishes the value of the unique individual creature and all of creation at large.

When a journey is based on emotionally connecting, it personally becomes an enriching life relationship. When one's passion is wanting to manifest it with all of creation; to become a part of the whole journey, it makes one's life journey even more enriching…

The only way we can truly connect emotionally is understanding what Unconditional and Self-Centered Love really is. Then make the choice for either side.

All other narratives are self-centered, distant and cold.

This Final Phase Manual Serves as Insights to Assisting Us in Restoring All of Our Senses and getting Our Core Numbers back to 10.

Note: *This is a work in progress*, due it being written in the beginning of Phase Four. Each reference section will be labeled as INSIGHTS following by a written number.

INSIGHTS ONE:

Going through each transition is like going through the birthing process. The wanting to connect, to the point of pushing through the birth canal journey. *At a point* there's no turning back. No choice but to press onward. Once in this "new" awareness; I consciously forgot where I just came from. But at times I subconsciously do; through premonitions, events and the feeling of being a part of something a long time ago...

This birthing process takes place through all the phases: **ONE:** In the beginning when we became a thought, then **TWO**: When we were spoken into a created thought (spirit), then **THREE:** When we were physically created, then **FOUR:** When we transitioned on and then **FIVE:** When we transition into being eternally physical.

Note: As we get closer to the end of PHASE FOUR, *transitioning on* will become less and less. To the point, not at all. All of Creation will "appear" to skipping *transitioning on*, to becoming eternally physical. In a *twinkling* of an eye...

Note: During PHASE FIVE and beyond, All of Creation are born eternally physical.

Each phase is complete. It doesn't end with starting to think about the thoughts of the next phase. Nothing distracts us from 100% appreciating, being completely satisfied and feeling complete without no lack anywhere. Before the next phase starts.

INSIGHTS TWO:

Replace the word for Death to *Transitioning On*. Death signifies the end of one's life with unknowns. ***Transitioning On*** signifies the uniqueness of one's journey in spirit, mind and body. Versus an abstract journey with questions about it, from those close by.

Walk by faith not by sight = walk by Unconditional Love part of the Spirit. Not by the Self-Centered Love part of the Spirit.

Your Word is a Lamp to my Feet = The Unconditional Love part of the Spirit is Like; a Lamp *guiding* me and being apart of my journey, of being physically and spiritually eternalized.

INSIGHTS THREE:

The higher the density of Unconditional Love part of the Spirit is, the more life becomes auto balanced. Our mourning turns to joy.

The higher the density of Self-Centered Love part of the Spirit is, the more life becomes auto chaotic.

Self-Centered Love part of the Spirit blinds us, from seeing beyond ourselves.

Self-Centered Love part of the Spirit dumbs down, extorts, exaggerates time; events, characters, environment, etc.

INSIGHTS FOUR:

Focus on Multiplying. Sowing Unconditional Love part of the Spirit, to reap Unconditional Love part of the Spirit. Sow 500-fold. Reap 500-fold...

We let go/release 500-fold of the Self-Centered Love part of the Spirit, to receive 500-fold of the Unconditional Love part of the Spirit. *This primes* our wells/cores, for more steady nourishing and flourishing...

1000-fold for 1000-fold, etc.

INSIGHTS FIVE:

Self-Centered Love part of the Spirit justifies a lot, if not 99.99% of the time.

The hardest truth to swallow is waking up to the facts, we've been lied to all of our lives. At this part of the Final Phase; we realize basically everything we were taught, is the opposite. This is Classic Self-Centered Love part of the Spirit, to keep us from restoring our senses.

The Unconditional Love part of the Spirit was/is moved by our desiring 100% "faith" in Unconditional Love.

INSIGHTS SIX:

I release the Self-Centered Love part of Spirit from my: spirit, mind, body, health, aging, life, passions, relationships, family, home, finances, financial independence, assets, community, city, country, earth, solar system, galaxy, universe and beyond...

to go back to its abyss to stay there, until **It's** Decision Day...

This is for me and my love one's part in this Final Phase. For All Creatures Great and Small, physical and those who are yet to be physically created. Together, finishing this Complete Process of Eternalizing Creation and Beyond. Plus; for the Honor and Glory of Our Creative Making Journey Friendship, together with the Unconditional Love part of the Spirit.

I receive the Unconditional Love part of Spirit in my: spirit, mind, body, health, aging, life, passions, relationships, family, home, finances, financial independence, assets, community, city, country, earth, solar system, galaxy, universe and beyond...

This is for me and my love one's part in this Final Phase. For All Creatures Great and Small, physical and those who are yet to be physically created. Together, finishing this Complete Process of Eternalizing Creation and Beyond. Plus; for the Honor and Glory of Our Creative Making Journey Friendship, together with the Unconditional Love part of the Spirit.

INSIGHTS SEVEN:

The innocence of creation trusting the individual; to the point of not knowing the potential harm (all of a sudden or conditioned over time) to their bodies will occur, *until its senses are being restored...*

Then being helpless to escape it: being chained, being neglected, consistently being scolded. Subtle mental and physical abuse; can be occurring over the generations, versus all at once.

What the Self-Centered Love part of the Spirit intended to destroy; the Unconditional Love part of the Spirit along with All of Creation allowed it, in the beginning to teach them what the words: Faith, Perseverance, Compassion, Forgiveness and Peace meant.

INSIGHTS EIGHT:

Nothing is impossible. Unconditional Love part of the Spirit IS IN: everywhere, every time, every place, every resource and every situation.

The more we see, the more there is. And the more there is; the more physical creation around us, can feel it…

Example: I see the *transitioned-on* Max around me and doing extra ordinary things, to let me know that he is. Then I see Cooper, then Smudge, then Betsy and the extra ordinary things they do. Max goes and gets others. To the point when going through out my day and night; there are hundreds if not 1000's of *transitioned on* creation following along with us, beside us and ahead of us. It wasn't planned. It was an all of a sudden. Boom. ***A glimpse of…***

Now with this accumulation, of Unconditional Love part of the Spirit within Creation together. It creates a higher level of Unconditional Love in that area, that it's not accustom too. So now the physical creation ***is more subconsciously*** aurora wise, aware of the contrast and embraces it…

And Smiles. ☐ A cloud of great witnesses.

INSIGHTS NINE:

All of Creations male and female companion relationships; will never experience their true purpose and potential, when Self-Centered Love part of the Spirit is allowed into the relationship…

When Self-Centered Love part of the Spirit is released from that relationship; then that relationship will become its own unique ecstasy experience in becoming intimately one spirit, one mind and one body…

In the same likes of the egg and sperm fusing together. The synergy has no comparisons.

The Self-Centered Love part of the Spirit ***will never***; be able to experience any of this, ***and or*** cannot even relate to it.

INSIGHTS TEN:

Silence is Golden. How do you say Silence is Golden without saying it?

INSIGHTS ELEVEN:

Unconditional Love part of the Spirit **automatically** "casts" out / **repels** / releases the Self-Centered Love part of the Spirit/ fear / etc.

When we release (*it's all we have to do is release*) – there's no binding, casting, commanding non-sense...

When Unconditional Love part of the Spirit is the size of a mustard seed; it can move a mountain of Self-Centered Love part of the Spirit, back into its Abyss...

The mountains of Self-Centered Love part of the Spirit must jump into the Seas of Forgetfulness / the abyss of the Self-Centered Love part of the Spirit...

AUTOMATICALLY! YUP. LET THAT SINK IN.... AUTOMATICALLY...

INSIGHTS TWELVE:

The Self-Centered Love part of the Spirit is like a rubber band. The farther it's stretched the more tension there is. The harder the human / creature hangs onto it; the more intense, frustrated and insane the human / creature gets / becomes...

ALL we have to do to be set free from it, *is to release* / let go of the stretched rubber band. And the rubber automatically goes back, to its original shape and size. **ITS That easy.**

INSIGHTS THIRTEEN:

Always Look at Self-Centered Love part of the Spirit as though it is: its last day, hour, moment and then vaporizes instantly before me / you / us / creatures / and all of creation. Everywhere. **PERIOD.**

INSIGHTS FOURTEEN:

The Self-Centered Love part of the Spirit's narrative: Two will be at the mill stone and one will disappear...

It's the Self-Centered Love part of the Spirit that disappears.

And... The meek shall inherit the earth. Oh my, this changes everything.

INSIGHTS FIFTHTEEN:

Qigong will assist in balancing the spirit, mind and body aliments; that Self-Centered part of the Spirit tried to subtly misalign.

Unconditional Love part of the Spirit is automatically compassionate, thinks of others' rights and freedom.

Self-Centered Love part of the Spirit is automatically putting oneself first by being: uncompassionate, intimidating and controlling.

The Body and Mind balances out the **Spirit** and the Spirit balances out the Body and Mind.

The Body and Mind completes the **Spirit** and the Spirit completes the Body and Mind.

The Body and Mind makes the **Spirit Personal** and the Spirit makes the Body and Mind Eternal. Personally, and Eternally Together. *Ok. That was deep. Stop and Soak it in.*

INSIGHTS SIXTEEN:

Self-Centered Love part of the Spirit's strength is five percent in proportion, to Unconditional Love part of the Spirit's ninety-five percent strength. Thus, the strength that Unconditional Love has over Self-Centered Love is greater...

But feeling the struggle within my body; it feels like fifty percent Self-Centered Love part of the Spirit, and fifty percent Unconditional Love part of the Spirit. Which is in the same proportion of THE SPIRIT. THE SPIRIT up until the end of PHASE FOUR is still, 50% Self-Centered Love and 50% Unconditional Love.

INSIGHTS SEVENTEEN:

Self-Centered Love part of the Spirit will work its way into any vulnerable network; to carry out its core-set to destroy all of creation, that was spoken into existence by the Unconditional Love part of the Spirit...

The Self-Centered Love part of the Spirit uses a predictable systematic cycle routine. *Note: It sincerely thinks, that no one is aware of its/this core strategy...*

Cycle starts with 1. Controls by Fear *(Based on Panic).* As Fear increases Panic increases.

Nosight of Unconditional Love.

Then **2. Creates Custom Ritual Routines** *(Based on Anger).* Ritual Routines "Appeases" Perceived Panicking.

Uncommitted to Unconditional Love.

Then **3. Installs Mental Slavery** *(Based on Revenge).* Mental Slavery "Appeases" Perceived Anger.

Hatred towards Unconditional Love.

Then **4. Destroys Family Structure** *(Based on Anxiety).* Destroyed Family Structure "Appeases" Perceived Revenge.

Introvert to Unconditional Love.

And finishes with **5. Destroys Creation** *(Based on Depression).* Destroying Creation "Appeases" Anxiety.

Doubts Unconditional Love.

Once the Cycle is completed. The Self-Centered Love part of the Spirit accesses if the Cycle met its goals, then realizes it didn't. Depression sets in, and the Self-Centered Love part of the Spirit shuts down...

The Self-Centered Love part of the Spirit snaps out of its Depression, when it hears All the Sounds coming from All of

Creation...

Then starts the Cycle all over again.

INSIGHTS EIGTHTEEN:

These are the physically fleshed-out versions; of the five characteristics of the Unconditional Love part of the Spirit, and the Self-Centered Love part of the Spirit...

Reference Table For Reference Convenience:

THE SPIRIT: When Creating Physical Friends			
50% Unconditional Love		**50% Self-Centered Love**	
5 CHARACTERISTICS	CORE:	5 CHARACTERISTICS	CORE:
Eyes: Insight	Faith	Nosight	Panic
Hearing: Accountability	Perseverance	Uncommitted	Anger
Taste: Love	Compassion	Hatred	Revenge
Touch: Extrovert	Forgiveness	Introvert	Anxiety
Smell: Teaching	Peace	Doubt	Depression
NOTE: The Core of Faith is Insight, The Core of Perseverance is Accountably, The Core of Compassion is Love, The Core of Forgiveness is Extrovert, The Core of Peace is Teaching.		NOTE: The Core of Panic is Nosight, The Core of Anger is Uncommitted, The Core of Revenge is Hatred, The Core of Anxiety is Introvert, The Core of Depression is Doubt.	

INSIGHTS NINETEEN:

UNCONDITIONAL LOVE part of the Spirit Characteristics:

Insight Sees the total purpose and the necessary critical details. Faith produces Insight.

Accountability balances all five characteristics out. Perseverance produces Accountability.

Love has Compassion for and with All of Creation. Compassion produces Love.

Extrovert reaches out to All of Creation to create new enriching two-way friendships. Forgiveness produces being an Extrovert.

Teaching to understand each of the five characteristics, relationships and creation. Peace produces Teaching.

SELF-CENTERED LOVE part of the Spirit Characteristics:

Nosight is Blind to the total purpose and the necessary critical details. Panic produces Nosight.

Uncommitted creates chaos with all five characteristics. Anger produces Uncommitment.

Hatred has zero feelings for and with All of Creation. Revenge produces Hatred.

Introvert insists on one-way communication and avoids reaching out to All of Creation. Anxiety produces being Introvert.

Doubt in understanding each of the five characteristics, relationships and creation. Depression produces Doubt.

Components of the New Five Words:

Faith: Child, Sight, Visionary.
Perseverance: Adult, Hearing, Accountable.
Compassion: Friend, Taste, Assistant.
Forgiveness: Companion, Touch, Creators.
Peace: Parent, Smell, Mentor.

Self-Centered Love part of the Spirit Creates:

Blindness vs Sight - Faith - Visionary.
Deafness vs Hearing - Perseverance - Accountable.
Flavorless vs Taste - Compassion - Assistant.
Numbness vs Touch - Forgiveness - Creators.
Fragrantless vs Smell - Peace - Mentor.

INSIGHTS TWENTY:

Since the Self-Centered Love part of the Spirit wants nothing to do; with the Five Characteristics of the Unconditional Love part of the Spirit, *it uses* those characteristics to destroy All of Creation...

Self-Centered Love part of the Spirit **uses Insight;** to control the vision of how physical creation sees its past, present and future...

Self-Centered Love part of the Spirit **uses Accountability;** to control the whole destroying creation cycle through, with fear.

Self-Centered Love part of the Spirit **uses Love,** to create conditional love. I will love you if you meet this list of requirements. Destroys the family structure.

Self-Centered Love part of the Spirit **uses being an Extrovert;** to convince All of Creation, there's too many of them. Ritual routines.

Self-Centered Love part of the Spirit **uses Teaching;** to indoctrinate All of Creation to believe they are stuck in an endless loop, of never being completely satisfied. Justifying implementing free roaming slavery.

INSIGHTS TWENTY-ONE:

Healing The: broken hearted, wounded, frail, famished, blind, death, diseased, mentally abused, physically abused, mute and all those in between; are really easier in comparison to someone and or creation that have transitioned on prematurely...

Their addiction of being 95% complete: lack in nothing, the individual's beauty and being able to physically create a child with their companion, supersedes transitioning on prematurely...

However those who have transitioned on prematurely; will want to complete their being physically created journey, by coming back to this physically created world during the Final Phase...

ETERNALIZING CREATION FINAL PHASE

As the Final Phase kicks in more and more of those who transitioned on prematurely; will be coming back to the point, all of them will be back by the end of the Final Phase.

Note: Coming back is in reference to wanting to interact; with those who are being physically created, and haven't transitioned on yet. *As the physically created restore their senses*; they will be able to interact with them, as though they never transitioned on.

INSIGHTS TWENTY-TWO:

Two sobering realities living in Self-Centered Love, *is fear* and *ignorance*. The fear motivates one to act on their ignorance; into a never-ending loop of mental and physical abuse to those, it interacts with.

INSIGHTS TWENTY-THREE:

WHEN 100% INMERSED IN THE UNCONDITIONAL LOVE PART OF THE SPIRIT; NOTHING WILL SEPARATE US EVER AGAIN. NEVER EVER, EVER AGAIN. PERIOD. Take a bath in that, and let it soak in.

INSIGHTS TWENTY-FOUR:

You can determine one's character, by how they treat animals and creation.

As the Core Number restores from 1s to 10s, the deeper the Unconditional Love interacts with All of Creation.

"Sin" and "evil" are too broad of terms, to explain what is going on and around creation. Replace *sin* and *evil;* with the Self-Centered Love part of the Spirit and now the explaining, becomes crystal clear to anyone.

INSIGHTS TWENTY-FIVE:

Activating Artisan Wells of Unconditional Love part of the Spirit can be done anywhere; location, individual, couple, family, home, friends, community, network of communities, planet, solar system, galaxy and yup at some point All of Creation.

INSIGHTS TWENTY-SIX:

Since we are not aware of our surroundings at a deeper level; due to our weaken senses, we "think" aliens first. And maybe. But as we get into this Final Phase; it's more stronger feelings of seeing those who have transitioned on and those yet to be physically created, we will be seeing before aliens.

INSIGHTS TWENTY-SEVEN:

Remember the Self-Centered Love part of the Spirit creates: Illusions and Concepts to mislead All of Creation, from the Unconditional Love part of the Spirit

INSIGHTS TWENTY-EIGHT:

Meditations are OK for Core Numbers 1 through 7. But when Core Numbers get into 8s, they will be less effective. Due to the senses are getting close, to being fully restored. This is when the physically created will begin to see and interact; with those who have transitioned on and those yet to be physically created. This seeing and interacting will stimulate, the physically created to stay in the NOW. Versus being distracted with the past; present and future concerns, that have nothing to do with the NOW.

INSIGHTS TWENTY-NINE:

The Self-Centered Love part of the Spirit seems to not like and or is repelled by some; plants, fruits, celtic salts, vegetables like: onions, garlic, herbs, spices like: cinnamon, etc.

INSIGHTS THIRTY:

Our Decision is Our Foundation.

With these accumulated insights; I'm convinced more than ever that the Self-Centered Love part of the Spirit, has flipped the whole recent narrative text references backwards. To convince All of Creation it has to leave, suffering is a part of the process and death is normal...

The same with all of the civilizations and their narrative references; so that everyone would lose track of its/this origin. It's friendship with Unconditional Love part of the Spirit, and this process of the Final Phase in Eternalizing All of Creation.

MY FINAL PHASE FASTING MINDSET

1. Multiply Sustaining, Strengthening in myself, my family, my love ones.
2. Routine Framework for my days and my weeks.
3. Stop the Slaughtering of Creation and Relationships.
4. Release all the Self-Centered Love part of the Spirit from my spirit, mind, and body. And my journey.
5. Receive all the Unconditional Love part of the Spirit in, with, through, around and beyond my spirit, mind, and body; same for my family and my loved ones.
6. Release Unconditional Love from my life to creation, to the point Unconditional Love is in all, with all, through all, around all and beyond all.
7. Unlimited Restoration is happening in, with, through, around and beyond my body; to all creation daily, weekly, monthly, yearly and beyond. Throughout my whole journey through this Final Phase.

Note: *These are just my personal examples.* Develop your own, to your own personal needs and desires. The IDEA here; is to set the framework for why we are pursuing, to COMPLETELY Restore Our Senses/Cores.

Note: The whole idea behind this mindset; is to set a foundation of ***dismantling and detoxing*** my spirit, mind and body from, the lies the Self-Centered Love part of the Spirit has indoctrinated in our lives.

TYPES OF FASTING

1. 1 Day Fluids Only.
2. 3 Day Fluids Only. Note: On the 3rd Day the body might clean out.
3. 7 Day Fluids Only. Note: By the 6th Day body might *completely* clean out. When done with the seventh day; eat ***very small*** meals to re-start the digestion system. Might need to start with soups first. Too much food on the startup, the food might go straight through the body.

   Suggestions and Tips with Liquids:
   1. Put a pinch of Celtic or Himalayan type Salts with micro-nutrients in water drinking.
   2. Have Almond and or Coconut milks. Put powdered nutrients in with these milks. Stir into; and or put these items into a thermos bottle, and shake them together.
   3. Have organic raw honey throughout the day.
   4. A tablespoon of organic Olive Oil *that was produced and **sold right from** the* Orchard, it was harvested from.

Note: These are just personal examples. Develop your own, to your own personal needs and desires. The IDEA here; is to set the framework, for why we are pursuing to COMPLETELY Restore Our Senses.

Note: I personally got a journal to document my fasting journey. I started out randomly doing 1, 3 and 7 day fasting. I done several 3 day fasts and a few 7-day fasts. I ended up primarily; doing one day fast per week, usually Thursdays going into Fridays. Example: Start Thursday after eating lunch. Then wait a little longer than lunch time on Friday to finish my fast, by eating Friday's lunch a little later than normal.

I've done this for just over five years now. With the one day every week, several 3 day fasts and a couple of 7-day fasts. I have basically gone close to 1 year, without eating food in a 5-year time frame. And my body weight has pretty well stayed the same.

Note: Personally; I have noticed that when I am more physically active in needing to use my muscles, I retain more body weight.

Note: My diet has been focusing on a vegan diet, for the last 2 and ½ years now. Currently as I write this, I'm aware some of the labeled vegan foods are really not vegan. I focus on roots, vegetables, fruits, soy products, dates, raisins, mineral and liquid supplements, Celtic salts, honey, etc. When can; I try to buy food products from the same places, that produce them directly. I stay away from chips, etc. that were made from dairy and eggs.

Personally, I have noticed a huge 180 in difference in my health. My vision is improving. My original hair color is coming back. My body weight has balanced out; between muscle and fat.

Currently as I write this, I'm in my mid-60s. When strangers try to guess my age, they think I'm in my late 40s and or early 50s.

The idea of going vegan; is to STOP the massive slaughtering of animals, just for the "taste" of meat. Just watch a few videos, on how they slaughter animals. **Horrible.** Hearing their screams for help. How they separate those just born; from their mothers and their crying out, for each other. All the food they feed to the animals; they're going to slaughter per day, would currently give seven meals a day per person on the planet. *Sobering waste of life, resources and energy.* Organic broccoli has more protein in it than meat, pound for pound. Sobering 2.0.

The Self-Centered Love part of the Spirit has convinced humans that meat is better, only to make the destruction of creation easier.

Note: As our cores start to heal and be restored; the justifiable reasons to destroy creation, for our survival becomes less and less. Our compassion sensitivity increases. *Example:* I find myself crying when I see a transitioned-on animal, laying on the road/side.

Note: As the Unconditional Love part of the Spirit grows in us, we are going to see All of Creation as ourselves. We are all the same **but unique**. Killing them for myself to "survive" nonsense, fades away *real* fast.

We will start to become sensitive to what the animals and other creation goes through; when being slaughtered, for our taste buds. Other examples as I write this: Male live baby chicks, are being grinded to a meat puree and sold as protein. Hearing cattle cry out for help; while they are being butchered, in real time. Hearing the pigs panic squealing out for help; while being gassed to death, in a shipping container. And the list goes on and on.

Repeater Note: The biggest attention grabber was; **ALL** the food they feed to animals to slaughter every day, would give every human on the planet seven meals a day. **SEVEN** MEALS A DAY. What a waste of resources, let alone all those animals' innocent lives.

Repeater Note: *The One* LAST BIG *kicker* for me; was watching a just born baby born calf, being pulled away from its mother. The calf was crying out for its mother; and the mother was crying out, and trying to get to its just born baby. *That torn me up…*

How could I justify that's ok, because I want to satisfy my "taste" buds? *That's Self-Centered to the core.*

Repeater Note: Especially when I found out there's more protein in a broccoli then cattle meat, pound for pound.

Tares Me Up Repeater Note: Then I started to realize even more, *Aaah…* the Self-Centered Love part of the Spirit indoctrinated me; to "believe" animal "meat" is better for me, because of the protein in it. I believe it without questioning it; because my taste buds convince me from all the "seasonings" they have to put on it, that its good for me…

Mean while in the background; animals are going through all this stress, just to be slaughtered for me? Their screams and crying out for help, just before their slaughtered. That waste of all that food to feed them; whereas if all that food was directed to the humans, it would feed Every human on the planet 7 meals a day.

Note: All of these Above Notes; are just my personal examples of how my life got more sensitive, to All of the Creation around me. As the Density of Unconditional Love part of the Spirit; was

OPTIMUM VIZHAN

getting stronger within my spirit, mind and body.

MY FINAL PHASE BREATHING MINDSET

1. "I inhale Unconditional Love part of the Spirit, and I exhale Self-Centered Love part of the Spirit." I do this until it's automatic. I'm priming my well that is within me.

2. "I inhale so Much Unlimited Unconditional Love part of the Spirit, to the point it removes all Self-Centered Love from my life." I do this until it's automatic. My Unconditional Love artesian well, is completely primed and flowing freely.

3. I'm inhaling 100% Unconditional Love part of the Spirit and exhaling 100% Unconditional Love part of the Spirit; so that Unconditional Love part of the Spirit will be in All, with All, through All, around All and beyond All.

Now my Unconditional Love artesian well; is flowing freely and manifesting restoration, greater than before.

BREATHING EXERCISE:

I slowly inhale until my lungs are completely full of air, as well as my stomach. I hold that as I'm slowly mentally counting to 10.

I slowly exhale until my lungs and stomach are back to normal position. Hold that position while mentally counting to 10.

Then repeat this several times. With practice my spirit, mind and body will become completely relaxed. This method can be used to either: fall asleep, control a panic attack and or anything else we need to reset our spirits, minds and bodys.

MY FINAL PHASE MEDITATING MINDSET

I was listening to these five songs before this book was written. As time went on, it was interesting to play/listen/associate them during these FIVE PHASES of Unconditional Love part of the Spirit creating friends. Looking back, it blows my mind how my spirit/core was setting me up to write this book with Max.

Note: These five songs are by Nigel Stanford; Album: Solar Echoes Disc 1.

> **Solar Echoes:** PHASE ONE. In The Beginning.
>
> **Entropy**: PHASE TWO. Speaking Creation into Physical Existence.
>
> **The Edge:** PHASE THREE. Releasing Self-Centered Love into all Creation.
>
> **Cymatics:** PHASE FOUR. Containing Self-Centered Love and 100% Vanishes/Self-Implodes.
>
> **Sea of Tranquility:** PHASE FIVE. Unconditional Love Spirit and Eternal Physical Creation Living Together. Forever.

Some Examples:

Unconditional Love; I want the Required Amount of Energy from Our Friendship needed to transform, restore and manifest:

1. **Financial Independence** in my life now; income streams, royalties, investments, job, etc.
2. **A Relationship** with a woman/man in my life now; with the same passions, etc. My Spiritmate.
3. **A Family** with My Spiritmate in our lives;
4. **The Needed Miracles** in my life now; for myself, my loved ones, everyone, everything, etc.
5. "_____" in my life now; for "_____",

etc.

All for the Honor and Glory and as a Testimony; of Our Unconditional Love Friendship, we have together. **Thank You** *Unconditional Love!*

Then grow from there to Join Our Hearts; as a community, as a country, as a planet, as a solar system, as a galaxy, as a universe and beyond as eternalized physical creation.

Sobering Reality is the top deceptive creature, on the planet is a human. All and or most other creatures are openly clear; if their compassionate and have Unconditional Love or confrontational and have Self-Centered love.

Self-Centered Love part of the Spirit has no rights to possess any creature and or creation. The only reason why it does; is because of the creation's innocents and or ignorance, of trusting and letting it.

MY FINAL PHASE SELF-CENTERED LOVE PART OF THE SPIRIT DETOXING ROUTINE

When we allow/absorb more Unconditional Love part of the Spirit into our spirits, minds and bodies; our lives begin to be restored, no matter what we do. This is what "health, relationships, creation, wealth, etc." clings to – if we are in need of them. "Health, relationships, creation, wealth, etc." are hungry to be set free. So; they ALL can enjoy this Restoration of All of Creation too, in our Creative Making Journey together.

Detoxing our spirits, minds and bodies from the Self-Centered Love part of the Spirit. The Self-Centered Love part of the Spirit has permeated; everything in all of creation, down to the smallest particles and life forms…

This starts with Developing a Routine; with this desire to RELEASE the Self-Centered Love part of the Spirit, to completely be removed from our cores. 100%. As our core numbers are restored back to 10; it automatically heals our spirits, minds and bodies, along the way.

THIS IS AND HAS BEEN MY SPOKEN; ABSORBING AND DETOXING "PRAYER" EVERY DAY, FOR THE LAST TWO YEARS IN WRITING THIS BOOK:

I Release (An Amount): <u>10 Trillion</u> Layers of 100% Pure Unconditional Love into All of Creation to: Penetrate, Permeate,

Saturate, Restore All of Our Senses and Flourish; In, With, Through, Around and Beyond My; Spirit, Mind and Body FOR:

Myself, My Relationships, My Family, My Assets, My Income Streams and My Shields...

My Friends and Their Shields,

All of Creation and Their Shields,

All of Frozen Creation and Their Shields,

All of Mother Earth and Her Shields and,

All the Highways, Byways, Pathways and Their Shields...

I Release This at the sound of my Seven Finger Clicks.

*Then I **physically** snap my fingers seven times then...*
Lock it ALL **in** with the Eighth finger *snap*.

Note: I started out smaller amounts in the beginning. It first; was twice as much, as it was last week. Then jumped to like 100 layers for two weeks, then 200 layers for two weeks. It would eventually get to 1 million layers, 2.5 million layers, etc.

Note: I personally noticed I had to do 3 to 4 weeks with the layers with ZEROS in them. Like 1 million, 10 million, 100 million layers; I would do three or four weeks in lengths.

Why? The higher I was detoxing the Self-Centered Love part of the Spirit out of my life; I personally would get depressed. *I then reasoned* the Self-Centered Love part of the Spirit; is so deeply ingrained in our spirits, minds and bodies at the nano level...

It takes longer to **"washout"** the Self-Centered Love part of the Spirit in every aspect of our spirits, minds and bodies. Our Individual spirit, how our mind operates and how our bodys function; all at the molecular and cellular levels.

Note: Clarification. The reference to Layers; is only a description to the density of Unconditional Love, for me to personally relate too. It's having nothing to do with the "science" behind the detoxing of the Self-Centered Love part of the Spirit.

Detoxing the Self-Centered Love part of the Spirit from our lives, is one's own spirit, mind and body's choice decision.

Example: It is the same with deciding to do body work outs. I start out small to build a body workout routine. Once I start seeing results with my workout routine, I get more dedicated to it. I modify it to get even better results. These workout routines; can be anything that I would enjoy doing, that give me the results I'm looking for. It could be walking, holding certain body stances, yogi, roller skating, etc.

MY FINAL PHASE IMPLEMENTING I

Tasks Mindset

NOTE: This space was intentionally left blank; for you to write down, your key point thoughts and action plan.

ETERNALIZING CREATION FINAL PHASE

MY FINAL PHASE IMPLEMENTING II

Relationships Mindset

NOTE: This space was intentionally left blank; for you to write down, your key point thoughts and action plan.

ETERNALIZING CREATION FINAL PHASE

OPTIMUM VIZHAN

Unconditional Love is Appreciated the Most When it is Lost.

Why is That?

TIME LINE BALANCED KEY POINTS

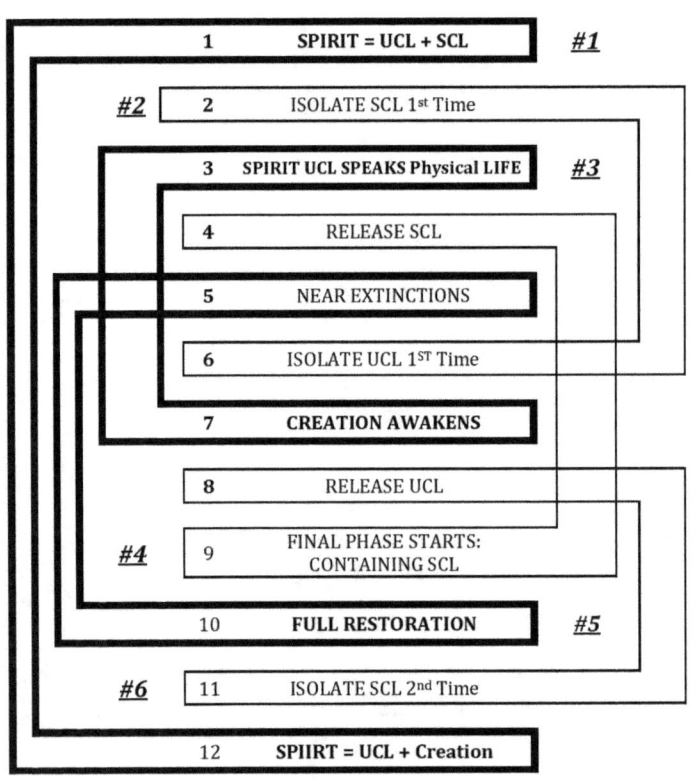

The following are summarized explanations; of what these KEY balanced points reference words mean, and why they are *key points of balance.*

#1 = 1 and 12: **1.** UCL is Unconditional Love part of the Spirit. SCL is Self-Centered Love part of the Spirit. These are the two Components that make of the Spirit. **12.** The UCL part of the Spirit successfully separates itself; from the SCL part of the Spirit and replaces the SCL part of the Spirit, with UCL Creation Physically Eternal. This Balances out the UCL part of the Spirit Again. BUT in a Deeper and More Enriching way, with Eternal Physical Creation Friends.

#2 = 2 and 6: **2.** To Make room for UCL Creation; the UCL part of the Spirit Separates and Isolates the SCL part of the Spirit into one location, its Abyss. **6.** UCL patiently stands by to balance out SCL being isolated. This allows UCL's Eternal Physical Created Friends to learn and understand the five words, on their own. This experience and understanding gives creation a Deeper Enriching relationship with each other and the UCL part of the Spirit.

#3 = 3 and 7: **3.** UCL part of the Spirit speaks Creation into its physical eternal existence. **7.** The UCL Begins to Awaken in All of Creation; as All of Creation pursues its Creative Making Journey together, in Restoring their Senses. At times it appears as "Miracles" to those close by.

#4 = 4 and 9: **4.** The first male and female humans with All of Creation's consent; choses to release the SCL part of the Spirit into all of spoken creation, so that they can understand and comprehend the depthness of UCL **9.** Humans choose to contain and isolate SCL part of the Spirit back into one location. Now that they understand and comprehend the depthness of UCL

#5 = 5 and 10: **5.** SCL part of the Spirit is ALL IN trying to destroy

all creation with multiple near extinctions throughout creation. **10.** Creation becomes fascinated and addicted to resurrecting, reviving and restoring physically in, with, through, around and beyond all creation UCL. In doing so, the SCL part of the Spirit is being isolated into one location.

#6 = *8 and 11:* **8.** Awaken Creation is now ALL IN to Releasing All of the Unconditional Love part of the Spirit. So that All of Creation can finish the process of Eternalizing Itself, with the UCL part of the Spirit. **11.** At the point UCL is in, with, through, around and beyond All of Physical Creation. The SCL part of the Spirit will be completely isolated as before, for the second time. Creation Released It from Its Abyss. And now Creation puts back into balance; by Releasing SCL part of the Spirit, from Creation.

Note: The *thicker* lines used to contain the balanced components of this phases; represents the UCL part of the Spirit's Strength, superseding the strength of the SCL part of the Spirit.

This is not set time line for this or that. Timing constraints yield different types of fears: Hurry up, Missed opportunities, Punishments, It will happen if stars align, Distractions, Etc.

These Five Phases balanced key points happen when embraced by the individual/creation and when their ready to. This process gently moves forward in baby steps. Sometimes the baby falls a few times, before it can actually take a step on its own. **Note:** Once the phase is started, its started. It cannot be held up, because some of creation is refusing to engage.

The key predominate constant is; that as long as the Self-Centered Love part of the Spirit doesn't yield to Unconditional Love, it has no choice but to concede.

Another way of looking at these Phases; is to look at them as a relationship, with a child in the womb. First time parents are at awe, make preparations for and wonder. That same child, now learns how to crawl for the first time. Both parents assist: are close by for; no rushing, excited for but when the child does it on their own time. Joy is felt everywhere with the child and parents. The same is for the first timers: standing, walking, talking, learning, interacting, accomplishing, etc...

It wasn't forced; it happens when the child is ready...

Then finding a companion themselves and having a child together, eventually for the first time. This is the Core Set of Unconditional Love Spirit, with these Phases.

Where are we in these Phases? At the time of this writing of this book/story; we are at the start of the Final Phase of Eternalizing Creation. **Relax.** Absorb and **Enjoy!**

The catalyst for all this Unconditional Love interaction *is ONE'S DESIRE TO.* The *stronger* the desire, the *stronger* the receptacle happens (the stronger the Unconditional Love part of the Spirit wants to be Apart of: With it and Through it).

The Unconditional Love part of the Spirit Desires a Real Genuine **Two-Way** Relationship, with Each of Its Individual Creation. Period. The Unconditional Love part of the Spirit patiently and compassionately waits, for Its Creation to want to reach out and engage with It.

The More We Live in Unconditional Love and Unconditional Love part of the Spirit lives in us; the more we think on and speak for, it will manifest.

Those Creation that have Transitioned On and yet to be physically created; are actively around us, all the time. Like Smudge, Betsy, and Cooper are still part of my life but currently not physically aware of them. Due to the subtle Self-Centered Love within me; trying to justify to me, they are "dead" and gone from my life...

Now Max transitions on and now I have to deal with it. I don't want another dog like Max, to replace Max. No dog can be like Max. All creatures may look alike; but all are unique and have their unique personal experience, that no one else has...

That's the friendship experience we have with Unconditional Love.

So now letting go of the subtle Self-Centered Love within me, I'm Consciously Aware of them and Interacting with them. But I cannot see and touch them yet, as of when writing this book...

Due to being consciously aware of, I can vaguely spiritually see Max. Then Cooper then Smudge then Betsy...

The more I have been releasing the Self-Centered Love part of the Spirit from my spirit, mind and body; the more our interaction with each other gets. It's becoming so regular at times; it's starting to feel like they never transitioned on...

I'm getting intermittent soft intros to condition my spirit, mind and body; to being receptive to seeing them and NOT be shocked, when I actually can see them...

The Challenge in this transition is; getting use to seeing, touching and interacting with those who have transitioned on and those yet to be physically created. To the point its normal.

Time Out: Why can't we just release all the Self-Centered Love from our spirits, minds and bodys the first time and get this one and done... done now? ...

I sincerely think that, when I'm releasing it from my spirit, mind and body. But the Self-Centered Love part of the Spirit residue is so deeply embedded, it needs to be **"washed"** out repeatedly. We are so "polluted" with the Self-Centered Love part of the Spirit; we don't know how "polluted" we are...

Example: I'm 80% "polluted" of the Self-Centered Love part of the Spirit. I release it from my spirit, mind and body. I feel so much better. But in reality, I'm now 79% "polluted" with the Self-Centered Love part of the Spirit. That 1% drop felt great in comparison, to what I was personally experiencing before.

Now; if I knew what 100% Unconditional Love part of the Spirit felt like, then I could have a better comparison to the change in percentages.

Slow and steadies, far out last one and dones. Period. Every time. The foundation is A LOT STRONGER. The detoxing experience is more appreciated. The wisdom attained along the way is priceless. There is no wisdom attained in a one and done approach.

The only thing; really attained in one and dones, is arrogancy. I did this and this happened instantly. There must be "something" wrong with you, if you can't get a one and done. Guilt. Hmmm. Sounds like something the Self-Centered Love part of the Spirit would say.

In the beginning of this Final Phase, the Self-Centered Love part of the Spirit is hanging onto All of Our Beings. Its goal is to hang as long as it can, to hopefully destroy us...

As the **Sincere Density** of the Unconditional Love part of the Spirit grows within us; then the Self-Centered Love part of the Spirit has no choice, BUT to completely let go.

So, if someone says; well, I did this and NOTHING HAPPENED, so this is a farce! NOPE. Odds are high, that someone was never doing anything *to **sincerely** connect...*

Think actions speak louder than words. *Think sincere two-way* relationships. *Think just by* that answer; it's giving us the indication the density of Self-Centered Love in that person is high...

There's hope for this someone; they just need to slow down and go in baby steps, so that it can be an enriching experience for them...

Versus a one and done experience. Which is also a strong indication, they don't have much patience for anything...

This person's frustration is like the baby that was just born, and its mad that it can't walk instantly right now. So, the just born baby is going to stop thinking and trying?

Summary Point: As more of creation detoxes from the Self-Centered Love part of the Spirit; it will make it easier for the next generation of children, from the original parents.

Example: 1st Generation parents get both their core number 3s up to 4s; then has a child. Their Child is next generation, starts out with a core number of 4. That Child gets its core number of

4 to 5. Their companion has core number 5. They have a child, which is now the grandchild of the first parents. Their child starts out at 5...

You see this example's pattern now. If each generation can get their cores to number up by one; then in seven generations their children, will be born with core numbers of 9 to 10...

Bringing this Example Home: It we are sincerely increasing the Density of Unconditional Love part of the Spirit in Our Cores; then it will get easier and easier, for the next generation. To the point, it will be automatic and the "NEW" Norm.

Hopefully that Makes More Sense, and Easier to Understand.

Footnote: If it warrants and I can, we'll be making Sequel Journey Update Books to help as well. Example: Volume 1, Volume 2, etc.

Ok Let's Continue, Where We Left Off: Now it flips to where we are subtly making progress; in the strengthening of the Unconditional Love part of the Spirit within our spirits, minds and bodys. We are getting fragments and glitches; of physically seeing those who have transitioned on, and yet to be physically created...

We take this process in baby steps. I **Strongly** *Emphasis* taking this in *baby steps*. By doing so, we thoroughly enjoy the process. And it becomes a Unique experience, that everyone else involved will appreciate that much more...

Plus; we'll be able to handle the fragments and glitches, in seeing them easier. The fragments and glitches, will at first take us off guard. We'll need to learn slowly, how to make them apart of our "normal" visual landscape. Example: While we're sitting, will be much easier than if we are walking and or driving around...

Or to simplify; learning how to master our depth perception while interacting, with those who transitioned on and those yet to be physically created.

Versus the one and done approach. If everyone was doing one and dones; there would be nothing special about their unique journey, with the Unconditional Love part of the Spirit. PERIOD.

Now we get use to the fragments and glitches; as being normal in our views, while still be physically connected to this physical world...

Eventually the fragments and glitches go away; and I can actually see those who have transitioned on, and those yet to be physically created. It becomes my new normal.

Next Baby Step. Reach out and start, to try to gently respectfully touch them. It will take several tries at first, with the 1st generation.

NOTE: As our senses are getting restored, the sensitivities will increase as well. As our sensitivities increase; we will need to adjust our spirits, minds and bodys interacting judgements...

Example: If I was nearsighted and dependent on glasses to see, to make better decisions in public. Now my vision restored, I don't need my glasses... Yeh!!!

BUT I lived with my glasses, for a really long time. I had routines around them. For the first few weeks; I'll need to detox from those routines, because I don't need them anymore. At times I might be apprehensive, to leave home with out them. So; I take them with me, just in case. It's a process.

We Need to Master Taking Baby Steps in this Process. Enjoying every little baby step, as though it was OUR FIRST. Do you remember how excited you was, as a Child Taking your first step? Your parents do.

After a few baby steps in trying to gently touch; those who have transitioned on and yet to be physically created, I successfully touched one...

To the point in this case; the one who has transitioned on, can actually see our facial expressions of joy on our faces. By them smiling at me; when I am gently touching them, proves to me that I am actually touching them.

BREAKTHOUGH INSIGHT: To help you start this. I actually put my fingers out in the "Air" next to me, where I think Max would be next to me. I gently and very slowly moved my fingers in the "Air," like I was gently rubbing Max. Then I said, "Max, give me a sign that you can actually feel me rubbing you." ...

And the first time I did this with sincerity; I got a one-of-a-kind sign from Max that he knew without a shadow of doubt, I would know it was him. This lit me up like a Million-Watt Bulb. Seriously...

GO slow in baby steps and enjoy the process. It's PRICELESS, Addicting and Enriching, ALL AT THE SAME TIME.

BREAKTHROUGH INSIGHT TWO: Yup. This is what I started to do, when learning how to be consciously aware of Max being around me. I asked Max, show me a sign that you are around me. Within 24 hrs. Max gave me a Physical Sign; that he knew without a shadow of doubt, I would be convinced he was there around me...

Example: Max always went out of his way; to do something uniquely funny with me, to put a smile on my face. He was a Master Tibetan Monk at this. SOOOO. That was what he did. That sign he gave me, made me smile like the "old" times. BUT BETTER.

Ok. Let's keep moving...

WARNING: *This gets addictive*... The more breakthroughs we have; the more we will want to take it, to the next level.

WARNING TWO: The detoxing at times *produces depression*. So again; take this process in Baby Steps, to manage it better. What's that saying? Slow and easy wins the race...

Currently as I write this; personally I've been at this for now, a little over two years to date. At first, I tried ignoring the depression. Personally, I couldn't. So, I slowed down. Versus being the Child that runs; from one new toy to the other, without really playing with the toys. *Example:* When doubling the intensity of Unconditional Love in my spirit, mind and body; started to produce depression, I would wait another week or two before doubling again.

As I continue this journey; this isn't about me mastering something and teaching it like, Now "I'm the GURU in IT" to teach everyone else. This is me sharing my personal experience with you; at this moment in hopes these insights, will help you and your love ones *uniquely* master it yourselves...

Make it your own personal journey, with your loved ones. To the point it's your families, unique Journey with the Unconditional Love part of the Spirit. That no one else can enjoy it, because it's yours and yours only.

I can't over emphasize; It's VERY Important to be sensitive, throughout all this process. Just like the Unconditional Love part of the Spirit, is sensitive to us. *Hmm.* Then gently move forward, just like babies do.

Hmm 2.0. This is why we all start out as babies. To remind us throughout; the rest of our eternal physically Creative Making Journey together, we are to go in baby steps.

We learn how to walk first, before we learn how to run. And now that we can run, we don't run everywhere we go. We're happy and contented to walk where ever we go. And occasionally we choose to run, when necessary.

Baby Learning Overview: The stronger the child wants to learn how to roll over; the stronger the parents are a part of experiencing, that season with their baby even more.

True Understanding only comes from Actually Doing IT. When we actually do IT, we appreciate IT A LOT more...

Watching cannot and does not substitute for Personal Experience. PERIOD. NEVER WILL. PERIOD 2.0

I can only breath in the NOW.

OPTIMUM VIZHAN

Unconditional Love is Appreciated the Most
When it is Lost.

Why is That?

HONOR AND PRIVILEGE

It is, was and has been an
Honor and Privilege
in first seeing, this first hand with
the Unconditional Love part of the Spirit,
each and every time. It still blows my mind.
It feels just like yesterday and now
this has all been penned in this book,
for all of creation to personally experience it themselves.
Individually, uniquely and enriching forever and ever!
This is truly an adventure of a life time.
An Endless Eternal Journey, with Unconditional
Love part of the Spirit to the nth degree PLUS.
With understanding of the past and the present;
we can all NOW move forward to together, in this
Final Phase of Eternalizing Creation!

OV

ETERNALIZING CREATION FINAL PHASE

Unconditional Love is Appreciated the Most
When it is Lost.

Why is That?

**THAT ALL CHANGES
TODAY!**

**THANK YOU TONS MAX,
FOR LEADING THE WAY!**

ROSETTA STONE OF UNCONDITIONAL LOVE:

Yup. This Spiritual Artifact that was hidden all this time, and it was only to be discovered during the Final Phase.

Unconditional Love Spirit part of the Spirit is composed, of five major characteristics. Each characteristic has five components. *When We become at peace* with all five components; of the five characteristics Unconditional Love part of the Spirit, then we can go to the nth level in our friendship with the "Creator" the Unconditional Love part of the Spirit. SERIOUSLY.

REFERENCE CHART FOR CONVENIENCE:

THE SPIRIT: When Creating Physical Friends			
50% Unconditional Love		**50% Self-Centered Love**	
5 CHARACTERISTICS	CORE:	5 CHARACTERISTICS	CORE:
Eyes: Insight	Faith	Nosight	Panic
Hearing: Accountability	Perseverance	Uncommitted	Anger
Taste: Love	Compassion	Hatred	Revenge
Touch: Extrovert	Forgiveness	Introvert	Anxiety
Smell: Teaching	Peace	Doubt	Depression
NOTE: The Core of Faith is Insight, The Core of Perseverance is Accountably, The Core of Compassion is Love, The Core of Forgiveness is Extrovert, The Core of Peace is Teaching.		NOTE: The Core of Panic is Nosight, The Core of Anger is Uncommitted, The Core of Revenge is Hatred, The Core of Anxiety is Introvert, The Core of Depression is Doubt.	

THE FIVE CHARACTERISTICS OF UNCONDITIONAL LOVE:

INSIGHT: Seeing. Macro or Micro Details. Insights of Doing Something without any prior knowledge and training.

ACCOUNTABILITY: Balancing. Follow Through. Harnessing One's Own Passion.

LOVE: Compassion. Naturally putting others before oneself. The Greater Good of a Relationship, Family, Community.

EXTROVERT: Reaching Out Beyond. Comfortable with first time conversations, anyone, anywhere and anytime. Feels at peace when adventuring out, to connect with new people.

TEACHING: Explaining the Details in Easy Steps. One on One. Entire Group. Understands the Five Types of Characteristics and Teaches Them Accordingly, from the Listener's Current

Understanding.

THE FIVE COMPONENTS/PHASES OF CREATION'S LIFE:

CHILD: Learning How to Spiritually, Mentally and, Physically Connect with Creation.

ADULT: Learning How to Spiritually, Mentally and Physically Maturely Connect with Creation.

FRIEND: Learning How to Embrace Each Other's Differences; while Enjoying Each Other's Company, Sharing Tasks Together, Solving Problems.

COMPANION: Learning How to Become a Companion in One Spirit, One Mind, One Body and Be at Peace with It; in Everything thing we do together as Spiritmates.

PARENT: Learning How to Spiritually, Mentally, and Physically Maturely Procreate a Child and Nurture Them; with my Spiritmate.

Each Phase of Physical Created Life; has All of the five characteristics, *within* that physical life experience…

Each of the Five Characteristics; has All of the five Physical Phases/Components of Creation's Life, within that characteristic.

All five experiences/phases must be physically lived through; to completely understand Unconditional Love part of the Spirit, to its fullest. And the meaning of those five words…

When I'm at total peace with each characteristic of that phase; then I will naturally be at TOTAL PEACE, with every aspect of my life…

ETERNALIZING CREATION FINAL PHASE

If there is a Phase that I'm not at peace with, then I will always be struggling with that area in my life...

Struggling characteristics are Panic, Anger, Revenge, Anxiety and Depression. Justifying my concerns, approaches and beliefs.

All five characteristics are always operating in one's life. However; we all have a *minor* and *major* characteristic, that is predominate in our lives. The minor characteristic is what we speak with. The major characteristic; is what we think of all the time, no matter what condition and or season we are in. **PERIOD.**

Example: If my major is INSIGHT; and my minor is ACCOUNTABILITY, then it's going to be easy for me to relate to others with the same combo. *If the combo is opposite* then it will still be easy to work with; but will need to tweak our communication, from time to time.

For Spiritmates to maximize getting along with each other; they will need to have the same, major and minor characteristics. No matter how they're feeling; going through and or season they're in with their relationship, they will always understand and enjoy each other.

To help dial in this understanding to the nth degree, this is a macro and micro version to each characteristic:

INSIGHT is operating either in macro or micro. Macro is overall vision, and the micro is seeing the finest details.

ACCOUNTABILITY is operating in macro or micro. Macro is overall understanding of completing a project. The micro is understanding the specific details of the complete project.

LOVE is operating in macro or micro. Macro is overall compassion of the relationship, family, child, friend, stranger, etc. The micro is at the finest details of compassionately; connecting within the relationship, family, child, friend, stranger, etc.

EXTROVERT is operating in macro or micro. Macro is the overall reaching out to new: friendships, communities, neighbors, etc. The micro is reaching out to new: friendships, communities, neighbors, etc. uniquely in deeper ways.

TEACHING is operating in macro or micro. Macro is the overall helping those understand the five characteristics of Unconditional Love part of the Spirit, Concepts, Techniques, Etc. The micro is helping those understand *the details* of the each of the five characteristics of the Unconditional Love part of the Spirit, Concepts, Techniques, Etc.

In Summary...

The Rosetta Stone of Unconditional Love helps me, locate these troubled areas in my life. As well as, in helping my relationships out. *It honestly assists* me and my relationships to move forward together; in our lives and relationship verses "seeking" counseling. PERIOD. The Rosetta Stone of Unconditional Love is our counselor.

**As the individual creature and creation
senses are restored**
throughout the Final Phase;
**they will obtain
their complete memory
of their journey,**
*from the beginning in the womb
of the Unconditional Love part of the Spirit
to current.*

IN CLOSING

From my personal discovery in restoring my senses journal...

Note: I was raised in a christian church going family. I was all in. Went to different denominations. As a young adult, went to church intermittently. Later pursued messianic judaism. Then a local church; that was focused on youth outreaches. Took a break to look back on all those experiences, and decided to stopped going ever since. Then occasionally study on how the traditional bible was put together, cross references that contradict and information that was left out.

Note: I noted all that, just to share my personal journey. I have no regrets of my going to church experiences. Priceless. Having those personal experience Makes Me Appreciate Writing this Book Even That Much More. Versus using what other people say, about their church going experiences.

11-13-2023: As I press forward in restoring my senses with Max and the family; with the Unconditional Love part of the Spirit, I'm beginning to think there was never a *"jesus christ."* Or as referenced by some, the *"Word Made Flesh."* ...

All of Creation is the Word Made Flesh. The Unconditional Love part of the Spirit is *Physically Creating* Its Friends.

Was there a "jesus christ" created for all of creation, so creation could be in physical contact with "god the son?" For this infinite + amount of creation to be sincerely respectively touched by the creator; through a physical "jesus christ." It would be a brief moment, then move on to the next creature... How could that be meaningful?

It wouldn't be significant at all like a 24hr 7days a week relationship. **None by far.** It would be a "one moment" aah ha excitement, but short-lived moment. It's quickly over and the odds of it happening again, would be for a very very long time away. I have to wait in line to have a physical connection with "jesus?"

If "god the father" created an infinite amounts of "jesus christs" then that would dilute the significance of the relationship, with each one. How would we connect with each other on/in a genuine way? If we all had our own personal physical "jesus christ." Would we be super engulfed in our personal encounters with our personal "jesus christs"; to the point our other relationships with our friends, families and spouses would be diminished too naught?

The more I think of it; this multiple "jesus christs" to make *him* more relevant in our lives, it would be more of a Self-Centered Love part of the Spirit thang, versus an Unconditional Love part of the Spirit thing.

Then the people who choose to believe he did exist; accept the concept that *he had to leave,* to send "the comforter." This "comforter/spirit" is to have, that more extended relationship to somewhat satisfy/appease them? Until they get to see "jesus christ" face to face... *In hopes* amongst all the crowds of All of Creation; to be the one that gets the "privilege" to be graced, by his few moments of attention?...

And what about all the other creatures that he made? Do the dogs get less attention than humans?

A "father god" figure over shadowing all creation; with a physical flesh "jesus christ" that becomes more of a power form of a "god", who is tolerable to "worship" because it's not a "many gods" concept.

If we were honest with ourselves; it doesn't matter if we serve 'many" gods or just "one true god." We are serving with/***by the same logic***. It's just uncluttered. It's a simpler life. "Less work" to do; in trying to "keep" every one of them happy, so they won't condemn me to an "eternal hell?"

With saying all that; it makes more sense there is just the Unconditional Love part of the Spirit who has a personal, private more emotional bonding relationship with each individual creature created entity, 24/7. That relationship motivates us to branch out on our own; to others who are having the same types of experiences, with the Unconditional Love part of the Spirit themselves 24/7. Be it; family, friends, spiritmates, and…and… and… yup, infinite+ creation, generationally through our whole Creative Making Journey together, forever.

This eliminates the list of "to do things" if I don't do, I won't be loved mindset. Of which would be something that the Self-Centered Love part of the Spirit would create…

christianity has been pitched as a more "higher version" of "worshipping" a "deity/god." "christianity" is the same process as with all the other "gods" religions. It's just simpler; less cluttered experience for the masses, to being ruled by fear under the cloak of "unconditional love." …

With this subtle fear in the background, I must submit to these "more connected" individuals "priests, pastors, clergy." Pitched as "gate keepers" to the "one true god?"

Where with a just plain Unconditional Love part of the Spirit **period**; there is "no control" of a "select group of clergies," who have been "graced" with the privileges of a closer connection to a "deity/god."

It's uniquely felt physically and emotionally in one's life, by restoring and producing obviously new/restored life, in one's life… the restoration of one's life being connected to and with the Unconditional Love part of the Spirit…

No one is in the middle of it; *"controlling it"*, *"judging it"*, *"guiding it"*, *"manipulating it"*, *"condoning certain aspects of it"*, *"questioning it."* … This sounds more like; the Self-Centered Love part of the Spirit's strategies, just honed down to a *"one true religion."*

And with that; a personal Unconditional Love part of the Spirit relationship uniquely blooming, growing and producing fruit of

Unconditional Love in and to others…to all of creation…

All of creation can embrace each other willingly, with pure untainted Unconditional Love. Period. As being eternally physical in their Unconditional Love, for each other and enhanced with the physical touch…

Without respectable physical touch, all relationships feel incomplete, that something is *"missing"* feeling. While being set free from condemnation; from anyone and 100+% embracing restoring our relationships with the Unconditional Love part of the Spirit, freely on our own. *To the point*; all of our senses are restored 100+%, and the Self-Centered Love part of the Spirit is *nowhere* to be found. *Period.*

It's the Self-Centered Love part of the Spirit's Day of "Judgment/Decision," to embrace the Unconditional Love part of the Spirit as well. **Not Ours.** We already did. Period.

In closing 2.0, I'm going to apply this message and knowledge to my personal life's journey. To be restored: in, with, though, around and beyond all my life. With All of the Infinite Generational Creation; with myself, with the Unconditional Love part of the Spirit, with my family, with my friends, with my spiritmate; that I have throughout this Creative Making Journey together.

My Awareness to This Journey Started with Max; and has been accelerating every day, after Max's Transitioning on 09-13-2022…

If you want to stay updated with this experience in our journey? My hopes are taking my personal restoration journal entries; and put them in sequel book volumes, as we go through this Final Phase together.

DISCLAIMER: These are just my personal observations; while being on this journey, with the Unconditional Love part of the Spirit. I have no desire to "reindoctrinate" humanity. If you think my personal views are incorrect then be at peace with yourself. It is your own personal journey and no one elses.

**NOW IT'S TIME, TO ENJOY OUR
UNCONDITIONAL LOVE JOURNEY!**

It's been an Honor and Privilege to have this vision, experiences with my Bestest Friend in All of Creation, "Maximus Houdini Koan."

THANK YOU, MAX!
MILLIONS. <u>SERIOUSLY</u>.

This Journey with You has been priceless, is priceless and no doubt will continue to be priceless.

I Love You Maximus Houdini Koan
with all My Spirit, Mind and Body!

I AM SO ... SO VERY PROUD OF YOU!

**It's an Honor and Privilege to be
On this Journey with You.**
FROM THE BEGINNING WHEN
The Unconditional Love part of Spirit Created Us,

To Now and Beyond!!!

You and Me
Forever BEST Friends!
In Pure Unconditional Love!!

Those prior words that are in bold on proceeding page; were the same words I would say to Max, while gently holding his face with both of my hands.

OPTIMUM VIZHAN

At the End of this Final Phase...

the Unconditional Love Spirit

is in All,

with All,

through All,

around All,

and

Beyond All.

FRONT AND BACK COVERS

Front Cover: The water flowing from the human hand; onto the dry arid ground, is bringing life to the young new plant. The water represents the Unconditional Love part of the Spirit. The water flowing from the human hand represents: the human allowing the Unconditional Love part of the Spirit to flow from it's being; to resurrect, to revive and to restore All of Creation. The arid ground represents, what the Self-Centered Love part of the Spirit has done to All of Creation.

Back Cover: Maximus is looking out in the distance. This photo was taken about two months before his transitioning on. This photo was taken from the video version. I was drawn to take this video; not knowing that Max was preparing us, for this next phase of our friendship…

The video starts out with Max laying on the ground. He normally lays on the ground to scratch his back; to do the back stroke, as though he was swimming in water. This time nothing. Then he pops up and takes his front right paw, and digs in the loose dirt with one stroke. He usually starts digging a hole; sniffs the dirt or something else, but never has he just did a one stroke dig. Then looks up and walks along the fence line; and looks out into the distance, like he is seeing something grand and spiritual…

A day or two after Max had transition; missing him like no other, I looked at all the videos and photos of Max. I took over the years. As I was watching this video; as I just described above. It became crystal clear, Max was letting me know. He was going to lie down; I would have to dig a hole, for his physical body. Then we would move forward; together in our friendship, in starting this Final Phase of Eternalizing Creation...

I got goose bumps on my tingling sensations; all over my body when I was experiencing, this revelation for the first time. It was fitting. Max from day one of our friendship; was always positioning us, for the events that were about to transpire...

He was gently conditioning me all that time. To prepare me for this big one; in him transitioning on, so that we can work together on both sides spiritually and physically. Together, guiding and or assisting all creation in this Final Phase of Eternalizing Creation...

Again Max, *Thank You sooooo Much for Your Beyond Epic Friendship! Seriously Bro!!*

What the Self-Centered Love part of the Spirit intended, for the death and destruction of all creation.
All of Creation Harnessed the Understanding of

the Characteristics of Unconditional Love:

Faith, Perseverance, Compassion, Forgiveness and Peace

to be in One Core Set:

In Spirit, Mind and Body

with the Unconditional Love Spirit,

as Eternalized Physically Created

Family and Friends Forever.

And EVER!

OV - See More Live More!

www.ingramcontent.com/pod-product-compliance
Lightning Source LLC
Chambersburg PA
CBHW050840230426
43667CB00012B/2077